TOLBERT'S
TEXAS

TOLBERT'S
TEXAS

Frank X. Tolbert

Doubleday & Company, Inc.
Garden City, New York
1983

Some articles in this book are based on material from the "Tolbert's Texas" columns appearing in the Dallas *Morning News*.

"The Boll Weevils" (published here as "Winning Wasn't Anything") originally appeared in the September 13, 1971 issue of *Sports Illustrated*.

"The Orange Christmas" originally appeared in the December 1980 issue of *Vision*.

"Ghosts of the Caddo Lake Country" originally appeared in the October 1980 issue of *Texas Homes*.

"The Girl from a Half-Million-Acre Ranch" originally appeared in the Spring 1982 edition of the *Texas Folklore Society*.

Grateful acknowledgment is made to the following for permission to reprint their copyrighted material.

Lyrics from "Mojo Hand" by Lightnin' Hopkins, Morris Levy, and Clarence Lewis. Copyright © 1961 by BIG SEVEN MUSIC CORP. All rights reserved. Reprinted by permission of Big Seven Music Corp.

Lyrics from "Evil Blues" and "Wonder Where My Easy Rider Gone" by Mance Lipscomb. Copyright © by Tradition Music Co. Lyrics from "One Kind Favor" arrangement © by Mance Lipscomb. Reprinted by permission of Tradition Music Co.

Library of Congress Cataloging in Publication Data

Tolbert, Frank X.
    Tolbert's Texas.

    1. Texas—Social life and customs—Anecdotes,
facetiae, satire, etc. I. Title. II. Title: Texas.
F386.6. T64   1983   976.4′063
ISBN: 385-08582-6
Library of Congress Catalog Card Number: 78-22820

To the memory of
TED DEALEY,
tough and talented newspaperman who,
also, happened to own the newspaper,
the Dallas *News*.

Contents

IV.   The Money Spenders

V.   Bits and Pieces

VI.   Under the Farkleberry Tree

Introduction

They Always Complain About Texas

In the U. S. Congress in 1850, there was debate over matters concerning the new State of Texas. Thomas Hart Benton, a senator from Missouri, complained: "Texas is too large. She covers sixteen degrees of latitude and fourteen degrees of longitude. Her southwestern corner is the mouth of the Rio Grande, a semitropical region of perpetual flowers. Her northwest corner is near a rooftop of the Rocky Mountains in the South Pass, in a land of eternal snow."

Texas existed as an independent republic from 1836 until 1846 and claimed all of the old Mexican subprovince of Texas. This Mexican western boundary of Texas followed the Rio Grande to its source on the continental divide between the present-day Colorado towns of Silverton and Creede, in or near what is called Stony Pass. From there it went due north to the forty-second degree of north latitude, which would place it around the South Pass in present-day Wyoming. From there it was marked on the north and east "by the old treaty boundary line as defined in agreements between the United States and Spain," and included the Arkansas River on the east.

The United States government agreed that Texas was too large and diverse. A real estate deal was made during which some of the northern senators complained that "the arrogance of the persons in the new state makes it seem that the United States was annexed by Texas." For $12.5 million in government bonds Texas sold to the United States its claims to all the earth in present-day New Mexico and Colorado east of the

Rio Grande, and also other valuable territory in present-day Wyoming, Kansas, and Oklahoma.

In 1983, Texas has hundreds of thousands of new inhabitants from the northern regions of the country. They complain but few of them leave. Old-time Texans, or Texians, as they preferred, were used to complaining newcomers from the north, such as James Pearson Newcomb, a native of Nova Scotia who became the editor of the Republican Party-financed *State Journal* in Austin in 1874. Here is one of Newcomb's gripes:

"Cheap land and great herds of cattle make the living easier in Texas while citizens in the northern United States suffer from the financial panic of 1873. Foodstuffs are so inexpensive in Texas that idleness is encouraged. Our gardens are running over with roses and vegetables here in January. Cabbages bloom. Beans are bursting. Even the red-nosed loafers bloom in the open air on the corner of Commerce and Main Plaza rather than in the back rooms of the saloons. Fishing is excellent in the pure streams. In Austin good cuts of beef are four cents a pound, and wild game such as prairie chicken, quail, ducks, geese, dove, cottontail rabbit, pronghorn antelope, and venison are sold in the markets at about the same price as beef. Our correspondent from the Texas Coast reports that the waters of Matagorda Bay cover one vast oyster bed. All you have to do is wade out into the bay with a bottle of pepper sauce. Oysters by the bushels can be harvested by waders."

It happens that the author of this volume was raised in the Texas Panhandle where some of the great cattle ranches were controlled by British capitalists. Many of these were members of the nobility or had "Sir" or "Hon." titles hung on their names, such as the Earl of Aberdeen and Lord Tweedmouth, owners of the Rocking Chair Ranch, managed by a relative of peculiar habits, Hon. Archibald Majorbanks; and one of my grandparents' neighbors, Sir Edward Gething; Sir Alfred Rowe of the RO Ranch; and Hon. Murdo MacKenzie, a magnificent old Scot who ran the 861,000-acre Matador Ranch.

Lord Tweedmouth complained that "the cow servants," as he called the cowboys, refused to perform tasks such as carrying in his luggage when he arrived at the Rocking Chair, although they would volunteer baggage lugging for Lady Tweedmouth, a member of the Churchill family. The Earl of Aberdeen was appalled when range cooks prepared beef over a fire of dried cow manure.

Cape Willingham, a cowboy on the great JA Ranch, became angry when the British proprietors of the spread in Palo Duro Canyon objected to having meals with the hands. Cape, later sheriff of Tascosa, complained to the Britishers: "You mean a man who can ride anything that grows hair ain't fit to eat with you folks?"

Willingham got his revenge during a roundup. The cowboys slept in bedrolls out in the open on fair nights or under wagons or tarpaulins when it rained. The JA's co-owner, Hon. John Adair, had a big tent and a cot and slept in pajamas. One night during a terrific rainstorm, Cape roped the top of the boss's tent and pulled it down around the Britisher.

The Adairs soon learned that they would be happier on the ranch if they had meals with the hands same as at all other Panhandle ranches.

In recent times Bill Shuttles of Dallas and I acted as escorts for a British nobleman who wished to visit some Texas cattle "raunches." He was Charles Fitzroy, tenth Duke of Grafton, Earl of Euston and Viscount Ipswich, owner of a 2,500-acre cattle and pheasant ranch in Suffolk, England.

We went on the tour in Shuttles' two-engine airplane with Tolbert as navigator.

The duke complained all the way that Texas "is a bloody desert." However, the hospitality of the 1,200,000-acre King Ranch on the Gulf Coast pleased him. We came in the spring when the fence rows of the pastures are botanical gardens and havens for birds and small game, guarded by prickly pear cacti rising in sculptured heights of as much as four feet and marked by military rows of date palms. And in the pastures were perhaps seventy thousand head of sleek Santa Gertrudis cattle, the cows' red coats matching the colors of perhaps two thousand head of quarter horses and thoroughbreds including one winner of the Kentucky Derby.

The duke was happy at the King Ranch because he was attended by servants, and he liked the good manners of the cattle kingdom's cowboys, called *kinenos,* and this direct descendant of King Charles II met a great scientist who specializes in "natural grasses," Nico Diaz, also a *kineno.*

We thought our nobleman might be happy at the East Texas ranch of H. L. Hunt, one of the richest men in the world. At the time Mr. Hunt had written and personally published a novel called *Alpaca* about a mythical country in which wealthy folks were given more votes at elections than people with few possessions. The duke left the Hunt ranch fuming:

"Mr. Hunt asked me if I'd like a copy of his book, *Alpaca.* I said righto, just to humor him. And the old bastard made me pay for the bloody book."

At the 450,000-acre Swenson SMS, founded a century ago by a banker from Sweden, Swen Magnus Swenson, in West Texas, the duke was somewhat puzzled after he was introduced to the foreman of the SMS' Flattop Ranch division, Scandalous John Selmon. Bill Swenson said:

"John Selmon, I want you to meet the Duke of Grafton."

"I'm glad to meet you, sir," said Scandalous John. "You're the first son of a bitch I've met with Uv for a middle name."

Afterward the old foreman would greet the duke each morning with: "How's it going, Uv?"

We were afraid to take the duke to the two hundred square miles of rangelands near Amarillo owned by the Marsh family. For the most visible member of that Panhandle cattle clan is Stanley Marsh No. 3, a young man with a reputation for playing pranks on guests. And some of Stanley's ideas on breeding cattle would have offended Grafton, a dedicated raiser of purebred Herefords.

A number of national magazines have carried photographs of Marsh's so-called "Cadillac Pasture." This is next to a national highway a few miles west of Amarillo. There are ten old Cadillacs, the vintage ones with tail fins on the rear fenders. Each of the Cadillacs has its nose planted in concrete and each of the high, finny silhouettes can be seen easily from the highway.

Stanley decided he needed some proper cattle for his Cadillac pasture. Incredibly, he was successful in breeding a short-legged Tibetan yak bull to some big range cows. The result has been some strange looking calves of a new breed that Marsh calls "Caddy-yaks."

Marsh's latest production in outdoor art gives the illusion that a big mesa in one of his pastures is floating in the sky. He calls it The Levitated Mesa. The mesa is in view of motorists on a state highway. Marsh built a board fence around the base of the mesa facing the highway. He then hired one of the leading landscape artists in England to come to the cow pasture and paint real-looking blue sky and clouds on the fence. The effect is quite startling.

This introduction was for the hundreds of thousands of newcomers to Texas and other complainers. This book is about some interesting Texans, but not the kind of personalities you are apt to meet in the big Texas cities where most of the northern refugees are settling.

TOLBERT'S
TEXAS

THE
MUSIC MAKERS

1

A Mojo Hand

When I first knew Mance Lipscomb he was seventy years old and a sharecropper farmer. Only, as he explained it: "With me it was more croppin' and less sharin'."

"Then I got me a good Mojo Hand," he said.

For the last decade of his life Mance was a nationally recognized extraordinaire, a singer with a saxophone sound in his throat, a master guitarist, and a composer of the blues, or of what he called "sinful songs."

He made frequent appearances, along with his friend, Sam (Lightnin') Hopkins of Houston, at blues festivals all over the United States. Mance and Lightnin' could draw crowds on a college campus like a winning football team. Mance told me: "Old fellows like me and Lightnin' is about the onliest ones left keeping our style of music in rotation."

One time in the Navasota river bottoms near the town of Navasota, Mance and I were following his rabbit hounds. The dogs were hitting cold trails, and they made harsh music of frustration. It began to rain. Mance called up the dogs and they leaped in the cargo box of the pickup truck. And we drove to the Lipscomb family place on the outskirts of Navasota.

Mance lived in an old frame cottage with his wife of more than fifty years, Elnora, and a dozen or so "grands," as the Lipscombs called grandchildren.

Elnora and a half dozen of the grands were watching television. So Mance and I sat out on the front gallery on hide-bottomed chairs, and we watched the rain come down, and my host hit a few chords on a guitar every now and then.

Mance and his friend Lightnin' Hopkins were disciples of one of the greatest of blues singers and composers, the late Blind Lemon Jefferson.

"I just knew Blind Lemon at the Buffalo Association," said Lipscomb, speaking of an annual musical gathering of black religionists at Buffalo, Texas. "Lightnin' was about raised by Blind Lemon. Lightnin' ran off with Blind Lemon when he was just a shirttail kid and stayed with Blind Lemon for several years."

Not many of Lipscomb's neighbors along Carlos Road seemed to know that he was a celebrity who drew big crowds to his "gigs" from Boston to Berkeley. His music was appreciated locally except by some "church people," his wife included. She objected to his compositions described as "sinful songs."

Mance didn't say he composed a song, though. He "estimated" a song. He never used the word "composed."

Lipscomb made strange and lovely sounds with his guitar, what he proudly called "my bottomless sound." He fretted the strings with the hasp of a flat, old pocketknife.

"A steel pick or a bottleneck don't fret as pretty as a pocketknife hasp," explained the old man. "Me and Lightnin', and before us old Hudie Ledbetter, is the last of the real guitar pickers. The rest is just thumpers." By "Hudie Ledbetter" he meant the master of the 12-string guitar, Hudie (Lead Belly) Ledbetter.

That time on the porch with the rain coming down he got in a kind of sad mood. He said he had been "estimating" a sad song for an album to be called "Evil Blues." The lyrics included:

> *"Early morning blues sitting by my bed.*
> *And when I want to eat breakfast*
> *Blues jump right out of my bread . . ."*

He said one of Elnora's brothers had helped him with the words for a song called "Shake, Mamma, Shake."

"Only brother-in-law done turned preacher and he say he ain't estimating no more of my sinful songs."

Mance said his long years as a tenant farmer weren't all bad. "Sometime I got to play my box (guitar) at church house parties and common school closings (he meant school commencement exercises), and in beer joints.

"Maybe I was lucky I didn't get to go to gigs in the air force (he meant airlines) all over the country until I got a lot of age and caution on me. Some of my friends were mighty famous when they was young. And some of them died young.

"Take Sonny Boy Williams. They never was nobody who could play the blues on a harmonica like Sonny Boy. But he got to be a big man up in New York City and he was stobbed four times until he died. And Blind Lemon. No one could sing like Blind Lemon. He got mighty famous and sold hundreds of thousands of records through those Victrola people, and he influenced a lot of people besides me and Lightnin'. Blind Lemon left his friends and somebody caught him on a dark street at night in Chicago and knocked him in the head and took his poke and left him to freeze to death."

Mance plays the guitar from top to bottom. And while he sang one of Blind Lemon's songs he played both the bass and the lead on the guitar. This Blind Lemon song started out:

"Mamma tole me, and Papa too:
'Whiskey and women gonna be the death of you . . .'"

Blind Lemon was buried in an unmarked grave in a cemetery on the edge of Wortham, Texas. In the 1960s, though, the people of Wortham took up a collection and put a historical marker over Jefferson's grave.

Lightnin' Hopkins was in Europe at the time and couldn't come to the dedication at Wortham. Mance was there, though, and so were five white musicians from New York City who went through some sort of mumbo jumbo involving sticking brooms in the earth around the grave.

"I didn't give no mind to those broomstickers," said Mance. "I sang a mournful song over Blind Lemon's grave. I sang one he wrote. It's called 'One Kind Favor' or 'Please See to My Grave Kept Clean.'"

Then there on the porch Mance began to play the blues and in his brittle but pleasant baritone he sang Blind Lemon's dirge, starting with:

> *"Dig me a grave, oooh wide and deep,*
> *Put tombstones at my head and feet . . ."*

"After that Lipscomb made it seem that two guitars were going instead of just one as he played a song he said was one of his own, "Mamma Let Me Lay It on You." He explained: "I estimated this song a long time ago on this same porch. A white singer named Bob Dylan must have liked this song. He followed me around to gigs for two years, to places like Berkeley and Los Angeles and he wrote a song to the same music called 'Follow Me Down,' only he changed the words. He mentioned me on the album, I understand."

Lipscomb had an esoteric language of his own. Sometimes he would say he "predicted a song." By this he meant he heard a "field song and kept it from being lost to recollection." He mentioned a sort of a sequel to the old "Easy Rider" folk song called "Wonder Where My Easy Rider Gone?"

"I predicted this song a long time ago. Heard an old, old man singing it in the fields when we was working. Easy Rider is a woman in the song, you know."

"Wonder Where My Easy Rider Gone" was strictly guitar, but next Lipscomb did one with lyrics. "This kind of a sinful song and I wrote it with no help from my preacher brother-in-law. This is a song about a big, mean fellow and his friend girl."

First he sang the role of the "big, mean fellow" in a deep voice:

"Blues in the bottle, stopper in the hand,
If you want to be my woman you gotta heed my command."

Mance then explained: "This kind of a sassy woman, the big, mean fellow's friend girl. She rise up in the bed and she sass him good." In a falsetto tone, Mance sang the sassy girl's role, first speaking of her bedmate as if he weren't there:

"Mistreatin' Daddy wake me up 'bout 2 A.M.
Try to make me swear I got no man but him."

Mance next explains that the girl has turned over in bed and addressed the big, mean man this way:

"Daddy, listen, and don't raise no san',
I won't as' you 'bout no woman
If you won't as' me 'bout no man!"

After that Lipscomb spoke of his recent trip to Los Angeles: "I'm mighty glad to get back on the Nava-sot with Elnora and my grands and my hound dogs. I sell a few of my albums, mostly to college kids. They listen close to my records and try to estimate my style. Only it don't do them a doggone bit of good unless ear music is in them.

"I found one white boy in California who could almost get on my side and find my bottomless sound. Only he was kind of twistified. Almost everyone in Los Angeles is twistified. If you twistified they ain't much you can do except get you a good Mojo Hand. And they ain't no better Mojo Hand than a sparkle stick, you know a limb off a farkleberry tree. The Indian people down in Polk County put a lot of store in the power of the sparkle stick. They say it's a Mojo Hand that can change your person and give you good luck."

I knew a little about Mojo. There is a high school football team in Odessa, Texas, with the nickname of the Mojos, and they are a good-luck, winning bunch. But I don't think they use farkleberry sticks for their Mojo Hands. I asked Lipscomb for his definition of a Mojo Hand, and he said:

"Well, it's a way of getting something or getting something

done or influencin' someone, only you got no hope of getting anything done unless you got a good Mojo Hand—like a sparkle stick from a farkleberry tree limb."

Mance said he had a feeling he was going to have "a bad sickness and have to go to the horse-pital." He played and sang Lightnin' Hopkins' version of a Mojo Hand song, and it suggested that the Mojo doesn't always work on some people:

"I'm goin' to Louisiana to get me a good Mojo Hand
To try and stop my woman from foolin' 'round with another
man . . ."

And this was the end of the song:

"I got me a Mojo Hand working but it won't work on you,
'cause you won't do nothin' I tole you to do . . ."

The rain had stopped. A white man drove up. He said his father was a lifelong friend of Mance's. His father was about to die and he wanted to hear Lipscomb play and sing for the last time.

Mance went off with the man. And I never saw him again. He died a few weeks later.

Elnora spoke a fine tribute. She said: "Mance and me never had much money, but we never had any unshared money."

2

Lead Belly Country

Near Carthage, Texas, on Highway 79, as many as eight hundred thousand persons each year stop off to pay their respects at the grave of Jim Reeves, the great country and western singer. He was born in a farming community near the grave site and rode buses to school in Carthage.

Milton Payne of the First State Bank in Carthage administers a generous fund for the maintenance and care of the singer's burial place in a landscaped, two-acre park. Gardeners tend the flowers, clip the holly hedges, mow the lawns, and see that the half-moon-shaped parking area is tidy. There is a sidewalk in the shape of a 25-foot-long guitar inlaid with artwork. Where the sound hole would be in the guitar, there is a circular medallion on which is inscribed: "Gentleman Jim Reeves. Time: August 20, 1923, May 31, 1964." At the end of the sidewalk, there is the high base for a white marble, life-sized statue of Gentleman Jim. He is looking very handsome in a dinner jacket and there is a guitar loose in his hands.

Reeves died in an airplane accident in '64, but his voice is still heard on the radio and his records still sell well. When last I stopped in the Jim Reeves Memorial Park, there were a dozen or so cars and motor homes already there with license plates from four or five states and from Canada. And I wished that my long-ago friend, Hudie (Lead Belly) Ledbetter could have as splendid a memorial at his grave. The great black composer, singer, and master of the 12-string guitar was born in Harrison County, Texas, on a shore of Caddo Lake and lived much of his life in Texas, but he is buried in a Louisiana churchyard about two and one-half miles from the state line, where Harrison County, Texas, meets with Caddo Parish, La.

In the Shiloh Church cemetery, near Caddo Lake, there is a simple marker for the composer of "Goodnight, Irene," "The Midnight Special," and other familiar songs. The gravestone just reads: "Hudie Ledbetter, 1888–1949." Lead Belly's songs are still played and there must be modest sales of his albums. There should be some money to give a burial site to match his genius. Who is getting the Hudie Ledbetter royalty money? His Texas and Louisiana kinfolks, including Irene Campbell of Marshall, Texas, don't know. (Mrs. Campbell, a school-teacher, is said to have been the inspiration for "Goodnight, Irene," and Uncle Hudie financed part of her college education.)

Wyatt Moore of Karnack, Texas, the old Caddo Lake boat-man, and I have been trying for almost a decade to at least get a historical marker at Ledbetter's grave. We appealed to the police jury (same as county commissioners) of Caddo Parish. Nothing was done until the summer of 1982, when the Louisianians finally put up a Ledbetter historical medallion in a public park on an opposite shore of Caddo Lake near Oil City, La., and miles from Hudie's grave. And his medallion is near a statue of a white pelican. Irene Campbell was present at the ceremonies for the Ledbetter memorial, and Wyatt Moore brought along some tapes of Lead Belly records to broadcast over a loudspeaker system.

Wyatt Moore and I still are trying to get a proper memorial in Shiloh Church cemetery.

I knew Hudie Ledbetter in the 1930s when he lived in Dallas. He had made some recordings under the management of his "discoverer," the great collector of ballads and author of books on folk music, John Lomax. Also, when I was in the Marine Corps is the early 1940s, I visited with Hudie several times when he was appearing at the Village Vanguard in New York City. At the Vanguard he often sat at my table between performances.

He told me he was born on his father's farm near the village of Leigh, Texas, in Harrison County and only a mile or so from the Louisiana state line.

In the country around Leigh, you still meet with Ledbetter's kinfolks and with others who knew him. For example, in front of the general store at Latex, on the state line, I became acquainted with Urin Davis, a tall, very thin black man dressed in a dark frock coat and striped pants and wearing a sombrero with vent holes roughly gouged in it. Urin was riding a very thin horse for which he must have some affection, for the horse was wearing an old hat tied to the top of his head with ears sticking out through the crown on the hat. "Step Lively suffers from the sun," said Davis, "and that's why I put a hat on him."

Then he spoke of Lead Belly: "When I was just a kid of a boy, I knew Hudie (he pronounced it "Hoo-dee," the way Ledbetter would have liked it) and I often heard him sing and whip his guitar. He still got kinnery here around Leigh and Latex and over to Marshall."

When he was young, Ledbetter was a member of the Lotta Church of God in Christ off in the pines near Leigh and on the Texas side of the state line.

One winter Sunday in 1981, Wyatt Moore and I went to morning services at the Lotta church.

The Lotta church members are black. Yet they welcomed two palefaces, Moore and me.

The church is now a bright white frame in the forest with a kitchen in the back and carpeting and acoustically treated ceilings. In the old days there were only some brush arbors. And Jesse Boone, an elder who plays the guitar and the washboard at services now, told me that Hudie Ledbetter "used to play and sing the gospel every Sunday here under the brush arbors."

The Sunday we were there was "Fifth Sunday," or the day when the Lotta churchwomen run things. And the lady who seemed most in charge was Beulah Boone, the piano player and leader of the devotionals. She is slender yet strong-looking and under her severe black hat there was a beautiful, black gold countenance and alert, kind eyes.

During the devotional she said: "Lord, God, You been so good bringing us up to this time. We thank You, God. Thank You for waking us up in the morning in our right minds. Bless Your name.

"This is the women's day. I am proud to be a woman. I'm satisfied the way God made me. A godly woman's husband don't have to worry when he goes away for a spell. You know what the Bible say about a godly woman. Yea, Lord! Thank You, Lord! Thank You, God! Thank You, Jesus! Thank You! Thank You!"

No professional choreographer could have improved on the grace of the choir members, mostly girls, in their slow dance-march down the aisle, from the back of the church to their elevated positions behind the pulpit.

They came two abreast. First they would sway and step through arabesque dance patterns and then one step forward would follow. They swayed together like flowers in the wind.

And during the dance-march Beulah Boone played a vigorous beat on the piano and her sister, Eula Boone, stroked a tambourine, and Jesse Boone sometimes played his guitar, somehow making banjo sounds with it, and then he put down the guitar and began to beat on the scrub board with downward motions. Meanwhile the two sisters and the choir director, Annie Love, led the congregation in a chant or song dominated by the repeated phrases: "Keep on walking, my faith! Keep on walking, my faith! I know He's walking by me! I know He's walking by me!"

When the choir was in place back of the pulpit, Beulah Boone called for "Sister Emma Dottie" to come to the microphone near the piano.

Emma Dottie, a short, squarely built, middle-aged woman with an air of command led the shouting and handclapping for a while to the beats of the piano, several tambourines, and Jesse Boone's guitar. Sister Emma had a little hat pinned to the top of her head and she was in a polka dot dress. These were some of the chants:

"I got the Holy Ghost inside of me! I got the Holy Ghost inside of me! I got it! I got it! Got it! Got it! We give You glory, God! We give You praise! O Lord, we're happy to be Your people! Sweet Jesus, light of the world! Thank You, God! Thank You! Thank You!"

Sister Emma Dottie went into a kind of flamenco dance, driving her heels furiously into the carpet and leaping straight up, yet never getting too far from the range of the microphone, and clapping her hands.

Some members of the congregation had turned into jumping jacks among the pews as the tempos of the handclapping and the chanting gathered speed.

Then suddenly there was silence except for some low moans. There was a sort of recess. We thanked Beulah Boone, and we slipped out of the church.

This was pure religion. But I couldn't stand any more of it. If I stayed much longer I would have been shouting and jumping and clapping hands like the rest of 'em.

We went over to Mimosa Hall, also near Leigh. The great mansion (completed in 1844) was built by John J. Webster, great grandfather of the 1970s owner, Douglas V. Blocker. Mr. Blocker, called the Commodore, also owned twelve hundred acres around the manse. Mimosa Hall was famous for an alcoholic drink of Mr. Blocker's innovation called the Mimosa Scald. It included among its ingredients Bourbon whiskey, egg whites, and pineapple juice. After a few glasses of scald, guests would take off for a wild, before-breakfast, cross-country horseback ride. W. N. Stokes, Jr., a lawyer, described Mr. Blocker's parties in the 1930s and 1940s: "Mr. Blocker would invite a number of his friends each Sunday to come to the plantation very early in the morning. The drink Mr. Blocker had 'invented' was served copiously. The Mimosa Scald went down beautifully on an empty stomach and was necessary if you were to participate in the proceedings that follow: a two-hour ride on spirited horses at a level gallop. We charged over trails and I never heard of any casualties on these wild rides.

"After the excitement of the ride, we were ready for brunch which usually consisted of scrambled eggs, country-cured ham and bacon and, of course, coffee. For years Mr. Blocker carried on this Sunday morning tradition, rain, shine, snow, sleet, clouds, or sun. It was always quite an experience."

"The Mimosa Scald is no longer on our bill of fare," said Douglas Blocker, but he offered us beers all around. The eighty-eight-year-old master of Mimosa said he'd have a "prairie cocktail," meaning a glass of ice water. Mr. Blocker was lounging on the glassed-in back porch of Mimosa Hall in company with a seventy-five-year-old black friend, John Marshall, and the Commodore's dog, a fat, alert creature called Mardi Gras.

I told Mr. Blocker about my project of getting a proper historical marker for the grave of Hudie Ledbetter.

"I've got some of his records. And I knew his papa. A good man. He lived on his little farm on the Swanson Landing Road, leading down to the lake from Leigh," said Douglas Blocker.

Then when we'd finished our beer he suggested: "If you've got the time to kill I can take you over on Lottie Road to talk with Sonny Man Gibson. He is a contemporary of Hudie Ledbetter and he might tell you something about Hudie's early days around here."

So Mr. Blocker and John Marshall and the fat dog, Mardi Gras, led the way in a pickup truck, and the rest of us followed in my car. Lottie Road turned out to be about eight miles from Mimosa Hall. And we happened to catch Sonny Man Gibson and his burly brother, Bubba Gibson, walking in the road.

Sonny Man is six feet, two inches tall and slender. He wore

very clean bib overalls and a blue denim shirt and an old felt hat. I asked him if he'd known Hudie Ledbetter.

"Man, did I know him! My whole back and the palm of my hand got acquainted with old Hudie about sixty-two years past. Hudie stobbed me. He stobbed me seven times. One time in the hand and six times in my backside."

And he showed me a deep scar in the palm of his hand.

He said a woman was mixed up in the trouble long ago between Hudie and Sonny Man. Her name was Mamie.

"I was knocking around with Mamie. And so was Hudie," said Mr. Gibson.

"You might say both you and Hudie was walking 'cross her front yard," suggested John Marshall.

"You right!" said Sonny Man. "I was young and crazy. Only about nineteen past. Hudie was a grown man. I got mighty jealous."

One moonlight night the young people were walking to a country dance between Leigh and Uncertain Landing on Caddo Lake. In the moonlight Sonny Man saw Lead Belly and a girl up ahead. He thought the girl was Mamie.

"I slow-trailed them for a spell. As I say, I was young and crazy. I charged Hudie, striking him with my fists. Hudie backed off and said: 'Stand back, Sonny Man. I don't want to hurt you none.'

"But I kept on cussing and hitting him."

Mr. Gibson said he then felt a keen pain as a knife went through his hand. He decided to retreat.

"Hudie stob me six times in the backside before I could really get my feet under me and move. About then I saw that Hudie wasn't even walking with Mamie. He was with another friend girl. Hudie didn't chase me. And he didn't deep-stob me in the back, else I might not be here today walking down Lottie Road.

"Anyway, I learned me a lesson that night. I learned not to slow-trail Hudie Ledbetter in the moonlight."

In the 1920s Hudie Ledbetter literally sang himself out of prisons twice.

He was serving a long term for murder when he appeared on a prison program attended by the then Governor of Texas, Pat Neff. He slipped a plea for a pardon to the governor during the concert with these words:

> *"Governor Neff, if I had you where you got me*
> *I'd wake up in the morning and set you free!"*

The governor turned him loose.

Hudie landed in a Louisiana penitentiary at another time and sang his way out of that one, too.

During my talks with the great musician at the Village Vanguard I asked him how he got the Lead Belly nickname. This is the story he told me:

"Well, I had this friend girl. And she was a duck hunter. That girl sure like to hunt the ducks. Well, one time she got mad at poor old Hudie. And she shot me with bird shot right at my belt buckle. After the doc pick out the bird shot I was good as new. But that girl spread the story around. And that's how I come to be called Lead Belly."

Morris Fair of Dallas told me about the time one of Ledbetter's wives sent him to the hospital:

"In 1938 or '39 I was introduced to Hudie. At that time he and his wife were living with his sister in Dallas on Bogel Street. Ledbetter had just returned from his first trip to New York with John Lomax, where he made some recordings.

"And about this time John Lomax's book *Lead Belly's Songs* was published. Hudie told me he wanted to see a lawyer so he could get a financial settlement on his records and on the book with Lomax. I took Hudie to my friend Joe Utay. (Mr. Utay is still practicing law in Dallas in the 1980s.) Joe agreed to represent Hudie and he got an out-of-court settlement with Lomax. The agreement gave Hudie four hundred dollars and all the royalties on his records. Lomax was to keep only the royalties on the book about Lead Belly's songs. Fair enough.

"Lomax had until about two weeks to pay Hudie the four hundred dollars. Hudie was broke. I arranged for him to get credit at a grocery store at Hawkins and Elm streets operated by one of my relatives.

"However, Lomax paid the four hundred dollars even before it was due. And Hudie celebrated with a lot of gin drinking.

"One morning I got a call from Bogel Street. Hudie's sister said: 'You gotta come take Hudie to the horse-pital. He bleeding like a hog. Hudie's wife done got upset because he's beating her so much. And Hudie's wife walked around him with a razor. You better come take Hudie to the horse-pital.'"

Mr. Fair said: "Ledbetter was then a rather fat man. And when I got out on Bogel Street I found that he had razor cuts in a circular pattern around his midriff. I called an ambulance and rode with Ledbetter to Parkland Hospital."

Hudie must have had a brave tolerance for pain, and maybe the gin helped. Anyway, Morris Fair said: "While the doctors were sewing up Lead Belly he was quite cheerful. And he sang some of his own compositions, including 'Goodnight, Irene,' in his natural, booming voice."

And when the Parkland doctors had finished with their hem-stitching, Lead Belly stood up and played on a borrowed guitar and sang.

"It was a most unusual Hudie Ledbetter concert," said Morris Fair.

According to Mrs. Winner Lane, one of the liveliest old ladies in the Caddo Lake country, Hudie was a great dancer. She told me:

"Hudie was one of the danciest men I ever knew. When he got out of the Huntsville (Texas) pen he come to our house over near Latex (east of Leigh on the Texas-Louisiana line) and Mamma made supper for him. I was a very young girl. After supper Hudie taught me to dance. Everything from buck-timing to waltzing. That night we danced round and we danced square.

"He was sure a dancy man, one of the danciest."

3

Lightnin' Electrifies People

Mance Lipscomb's best friend, Sam (Lightnin') Hopkins, told me: "I took up with Blind Lemon Jefferson at the Buffalo Association in Buffalo, Texas, when I was about eight years old. Ever since I been whipping a guitar and singing and making songs. Blind Lemon said when I played and sang I electrified people. He was the one that started calling me Lightnin'."

Hopkins, who died in 1982, lived in Houston most of his life and he was one of that town's real celebrities. For example, when the Beatles used to come to Houston as a group, Lightnin' was often the first person they wished to see. He seemed to be the only personality in Houston in whom they showed much interest.

"Reason for that," said Hopkins, "was that before the Beatles amounted to much, I gave them a lot of help with the guitar. They said I sort of set their beat.

"Knowing the Beatles was the best thing that happened to me on European tours. For I got jived out of a lot of money in Europe."

Hopkins hated telephones. When I asked for his phone number, he gave me a business card of his personal physician.

"You call the doctor man's office and leave your number," he said.

There was another procedure which I went through most often involving a Chinese grocery store across Gray Street from Lightnin's apartment house in Houston's black ghetto. I would leave a note at the grocery store and then come back in an hour and the store owner would inform me whether or not

Mr. Hopkins was at home and whether or not he wished to see me. The last time I was greeted by Lightnin's young and beautiful wife, Antoinette.

Antoinette said her husband was preparing to leave for some concerts in other states, but he had time for some drinks, in this case sipping gin followed by a swallow of cold beer.

The apartment was well furnished. On the walls were some oil paintings, including one of Hopkins. Lightnin' was medium tall and wiry and his age in 1980 was supposed to be 68.

No one seemed sure about Lightnin's age, including Lightnin'.

Except to say that at age eight he became a street singer and followed Blind Lemon to "Deep Ellum" (Elm) in Dallas and other gathering places for black musicians, Hopkins was reticent about his personal chronology.

Mance had told me he thought that his friend was born in Centerville, Texas (near Buffalo and also in Leon County), in 1912. I asked Hopkins about this, and he gave me a somewhat evasive answer:

"Well, Centerville was where I grew up to know myself as a boy."

Same as Mance, Lightnin' didn't "compose" songs. Rather he "made them." He said he sometimes thought up a song right in the middle of a concert or nightclub appearance.

"It's people that move me," he said. "I can't play and sing and make up songs to no blank walls. I needs people like a preacher needs his amens. If'n a real good preacher don't get no amens, he can't preach."

4

Jules Bledsoe's "Sad Stone"

It was dismaying to see what had happened to the grave of Jules Bledsoe, 1899–1943.

He was once one of the great musical stars of the New York stage. He is buried in a weed-choked acreage of an old cemetery in Waco. Nearby are the soaring patterns of an elevated freeway interchange.

I had to pull weeds for fifteen minutes before I could read what was on the gravestone beside Jules's name and the years when he was born and when he died. Under his sparse vital statistics was carved the legend "Ol' Man River," and under that some of the music and lyrics from the Jerome Kern song.

An elderly black man who lives near the cemetery told me later: "You can't see the sad stones (gravestones) for the weeds. Seems they just bury people and forget them in that old graveyard."

Jules Bledsoe was a magnificent personality with a deep, echoing, mellow voice. His most memorable role was as Joe in the original Broadway production of the play which had Jerome Kern's most memorable score, *Show Boat*.

The black singer from Waco became a personal friend of Jerome Kern. And the composer wrote one of the songs for *Show Boat* with the voice of Jules Bledsoe in mind. The song was, of course, "Ol' Man River" with lyrics by Oscar Hammerstein II.

At least, Jules has an imaginative monument with the title

and some of the music carved in the white stone. Only the grave needs maintenance, weeds chopped regularly. Or as Blind Lemon Jefferson expressed it in his song: "One Kind Favor: Please See to My Grave Kept Clean."

5

How Did Blind Lemon Die?

Playboy magazine wrote: "The immortal black musician, Blind Lemon Jefferson, died while waiting for a streetcar in Chicago."

This is a flippant reference to a mystery.

Mr. Jefferson, a native of farm country near Wortham, Texas, wrote poetic blues songs. And he had a haunting, remarkably powerful and clear voice. His friend, Mance Lipscomb, described Blind Lemon's voice for me:

"He would break time and hit four or five beats before he caught up with time. By time I mean rhythm. When I was a boy I would sit around and listen to Blind Lemon and try to estimate his style of singing. But I never could, except he sang loud and clear. When concert singing, he sounded like he was singing out in the fields. You could hear him for a half mile. They didn't need no loudspeaker at Blind Lemon's gigs."

Uel L. Davis, Jr., the Wortham postmaster, was the chairman of a committee which raised the money in 1965 and placed a historical marker over the previously unmarked grave of Blind Lemon Jefferson in a little cemetery on the Van Hook Stubbs ranch on the outskirts of Wortham.

Uel Davis has a collection of Jefferson's records, including the most recent album called "Immortal Blind Lemon" (Milestone Records 2204) and some old 78s with titles such as "Lowdown Mojo Hand Blues" and "Piney Woods Moneyed Mamma" and "Waiting on the Cairo Street Corner."

"Just how did he die?" I asked Uel Davis.

"I wish I knew," he replied. "Before we raised the historical marker I wrote to the Chicago and Cook County governments and tried to get Jefferson's death certificate. They sent me a good-sized bill for the research but said they couldn't find a death certificate."

When I told this to Blind Lemon's disciples, Lightnin' Hopkins and Mance Lipscomb, Mance said, bitterly: "To them Chicago polices Blind Lemon was just another black man found dead on the street. They didn't figure any court record was needed."

In 1965 the historical marker was dedicated over Jefferson's grave. The ceremonies took place in a rainstorm with thunderous sound effects. Someone held an umbrella over Mance Lipscomb as he sang Blind Lemon's composition, "One Kind Favor: Please See to My Grave Kept Clean."

Uel Davis had a clipping from a story in the weekly Wortham newspaper about Jefferson's funeral on New Year's Day, 1930. The story indicated that his funeral on that bleak day in 1930 didn't go the way he had asked in the song "One Kind Favor." For example, Blind Lemon wanted:

> *"Two white horses, side by side,*
> *Take me on my farewell ride . . ."*

There was pomp and ceremony, although no white horses, when Mance sang over the grave thirty-five years after the funeral:

> *"When you hear church bells gong*
> *It will be my funeral song . . ."*

Mance fretted the neck of his guitar with the hasp of his pocketknife for sounds very like church bells as he sang:

> *"Dig me a grave, oooh wide and deep,*
> *Put tombstones at my head and feet . . ."*

The rains stopped. And after the formal ceremony was over, Mance played some of Blind Lemon's "sinful songs" such as "Brownskin Blues" which has this verse:

" 'Fess up, Brown, where you stay last night?
'Fess up, Brown, where you stay last night?
Your hair's messed up and your talk ain't right . . ."

Still there is that nagging mystery: how did Blind Lemon die? And why?

Mance Lipscomb said: "I was just sharecropping down on the Navasot, and it was hard times in the winter of 1929–1930. But the way I heard it, Blind Lemon had just been paid off a lot of money in cash by two big record companies and he wanted to go to the depot there in Chicago and catch a train home. Being a blind man he needed someone to guide him to the depot. Whoever started out guiding him didn't finish the job. Anyway somebody knocked him in the head and took his poke with all that record money in it and left my friend on the cold, cold street to freeze to death."

"One of the record companies apparently paid to have Jefferson's body sent back to Wortham," said Uel Davis.

Blind Lemon's records still sell. Who gets the money due his estate? No one seems to know in Wortham.

DAILY LIVING

6

Cooking for a President

"It got mighty wearisome cooking with them FBIs watching every move I made," said Jessie Fantroy. "And if President Johnson even got the hiccups, it was sort of my fault. I was responsible for every mouthful the President had sometimes for quite a spell."

For sixteen years, Mrs. Fantroy was the chef at Lyndon Johnson's hideaway at Lake Lyndon B. Johnson, originally Granite Shoals Lake in the Texas Hill Country.

Now this charming, youthful-looking black woman is the chief cook in the employee's cafe in a unique financial institution, the Cow Pasture Bank in the village of Rio Vista in Johnson County, Texas.

"It's a lot nicer cooking for bankers with no FBIs snooping around in my kitchen," she said, meaning the secret service people when she spoke of "FBIs."

She said that Lyndon Johnson was an appreciative boss and easy to cook for. "The trouble really started for me when he made President. They was sometimes eight or ten of them FBIs sniffing and tasting all the ingredients in my cookery."

She said when she went to Marble Falls or Llano to shop for supplies she was supervised "and when I was in town I wasn't supposed to talk with anyone except to order things. People I know got to thinking I was stuck-up or rude. And when I got back to the lake house all my supplies was checked over again."

Mrs. Fantroy said she likes to read in bed. "But if I'd get to reading late at night one of them FBIs might rap on my bedroom door and ask if everything was all right. I got so sometimes I would lie down in the bathtub and read so they couldn't spy that my light was on late at night."

She said she "got to feeling like one of them tasters for the old-time kings. I didn't do no drink testing, though. I talked my way out of being the bartender. I said it was against my religion to serve anyone, even the President of the United States, any drinks with spirits in them. And that's the truth."

She cooked for dozens of foreign dignitaries. The one she remembers most vividly was Chancellor Ludwig Erhard of West Germany.

"I was told to get some Texas Hill Country smoked sausage and other German-like food for the chancellor's breakfast," she said. "Only when I cooked and brought in the German-like food he started yelling at me in German."

One of the chancellor's aides explained his rantings to Mrs. Fantroy: "He says to take this stuff away. He wants some bacon and eggs."

After sixteen years she said she resigned reluctantly because she was told she would have to go to Washington and cook the President's favorite Texas foods in the White House.

The Cow Pasture Bank has a cookbook with many of Mrs. Fantroy's recipes in them.

7

The Peyote Dealer

Two Navajo Indians, Mr. and Mrs. Mike Cowboy of Chicken Bite, Arizona, had just left Amada Cardenas' campgrounds when I stopped off to visit with this remarkable woman.

Mrs. Cardenas is a licensed dealer in peyote buttons. And since 1933 she has provided free camping for Indians who come to her little rancho on the outskirts of Mirando City, Texas, to purchase her produce, the dollar-sized cylindroidal fruit of a cactus with the botanical title of *Lophophora williamsii* (Lem.) J. Coult. Peyote.

Peyote grows in very limited areas now in the United States, most profusely along the Rio Grande shores near Laredo—Mirando City is about twenty-five miles from Laredo—in an oil field. The fleshy cacti buttons are classified as a hallucinogenic drug and are used as a sacrament during all-night prayer vigils by about 300,000 members of the Native American Church. Only card-carrying members of the Native American Church, required to have not less than twenty-five percent Indian blood, are permitted to buy the drug, and only from licensed dealers such as Mrs. Cardenas.

Alongside Amada Cardenas' white cottage are two smaller houses in which Indians can bunk. And perhaps in part because of Mrs. Cardenas' hospitality, Mirando City has become a kind of magnet for Native American Church religionists who believe peyote is eaten to absorb God's spirit in much the same manner that other Christian faiths take the sacrament through bread and wine.

Decades ago the Utes from Utah left some lodgepoles there and these are used to raise teepees in which the Indians eat peyote and drum and pray at night.

"I have never eaten peyote," said Amada Cardenas. "My Indians say that the buttons produce a sense of well-being and closeness to God. Never have I had any of them misbehave while camped here. They are good Christians, same as me, and their faith holds them up."

Since she won't take money for camping, the Indians leave presents, usually artistic crafts. Her little house is a kind of museum of Indian crafts. She is an honorary member of a score of tribes.

Her visitors register. I looked at a list of the Indians who had camped there in recent times after my visit and they included members of these tribes or nations: Sioux, Cheyenne, Comanche, Kiowa, Kickapoo, Ute, Navajo, Arapaho. Some have unusual names by paleface standards, such as Harvey Holliday from Mexican Hat, Utah, and John White Shirt from Colony, Oklahoma, and Jimmy Hummingbird of Hardin, Montana, and Winston Churchill (no kidding) from Rough Rock, Arizona, and Ruth Many Goats from Road End, New Mexico, and Billy Arizona, Jr., from Chicken Bite, Arizona.

Mrs. Cardenas said: "When my late husband, Claudio, and I first began to sell this sacrament we would offer a thousand buttons for $2.50, and there was no government regulation. Now I hear that some dealers are charging as much as $80 for a thousand buttons. And some of these Indians, after say a trip all the way from Montana, are too poor to buy their sacrament for $60 to $80 when they get here. Right now I have no peyote. But I have some peyote growing in my yard. When I have no buttons I still let my Indians camp in the yard and pray over the living plants. They say it is better than no sacrament at all."

Government regulations now bewilder both the card-carrying religionists and the peyote dealers, who must be licensed by the federal government. The government won't grant financial aid for making improvements, such as damning streams, to ranchers who permit peyote to be harvested on their land. As a result licensed dealers often have to get the buttons in devious ways, such as from cowboys who moonlight for illicit harvests. And prices are inflated with each crop.

"Heepies (Hippies) cause much trouble around here," said Amada. "They come from as far away as California and New York. They are always trying to get some peyote. They can't buy it. So they go into pastures and steal it. And this has caused many ranchers to lock their pasture gates."

On Mrs. Cardenas' living room wall, among all the artistic examples of Indian crafts, there is a large metal plaque which reads:

"At the annual convention of the Native American Church in Window Rock, Arizona, the Navajo Nation gratefully acknowledges the understanding of Amada S. Cardenas in providing all of the resources needed in the legal use of peyote as a sacrament in the services of the Native American Church."

The Navajos came by car not only to get a year's supply of peyote but also to carry Mrs. Cardenas to the ceremonies at Window Rock—and to bring her back to Mirando City. Another time she got a round trip to Gallup in New Mexico because the Navajos wanted her to see the new cathedral of their church there.

The prayer drums sound many nights out of the year at Amada's little compound on the edge of Mirando City. She said of this: "I don't mind the drums at night. I sleep with drums. For I know that prayers are being said for me by my Indians."

8

Some Slaves I've Known

One of the many former slaves I knew was a tall, dignified fellow who called himself Will Satisfied-He-Done-Got-Away. What he described as his "slave name" was Will Scott.

He got his meager pension check made out to Will Scott. His friends called him Satisfied.

He said he was about 111 years old at a time when I was bringing him pots of chili con carne. He said: "I'm just a pig for chili. If I live to 200 I won't get my fill of chili."

Satisfied lived in a drafty shack at the corner of Landis and North streets near the Corinth Street crossing of the Trinity River in Dallas.

He said his parents got the name Scott because his mother and father were wedding gifts during slavery times in Louisiana when a much married belle became Mrs. Scott.

At the end of the States War, federal troops overran Louisiana. And Satisfied's father, Moses Scott, led the families on a long walk into Texas. Satisfied said his father and mother were completely illiterate. "They couldn't count to five."

He said that near Bastrop, Texas, "We come on some Yankee soldiers who told us we was free. We got registered I guess so my papa and mama could vote. None of us knew when we was borned or our ages. The Yankees gave us all February 4 for a birthday and they estimated our ages.

"They guess me about ten, I think they guess too low because I got to be a man too soon after that. But anyway that's my age on the book, and the one on which I get my 'long dividity,'" meaning his social security payments.

There were efforts to put Satisfied in a rest home. He resisted this: "I don't want to live in no poorhouse. I can sustain myself. I never drank no spirits. I don't even drink coffee. I don't smoke and I don't dip or chew. I don't bother nobody. I want to live alone. I don't want them cats that come to live with me. Them cats don't belong to me. They just come here and I share my rations with them because they are living creatures and I feel sorry for them."

He worked as a yardman until he was more than one hundred by rough reckoning. He was a yardman in Dallas for more than eighty years.

"I worked the yard for a nice Dallas lady who took time to learn me to read simple words. I kept on asking her what other words in print meant. Once she or other folks told me the meaning of a word I remembered that word for good. It took me a long time, but finally they come the blessed day when I could read the Bible through and through."

At age 111 he read the Bible without the help of glasses. He appreciated my chili con carne gifts. And he said: "I can't get me enough chili."

Camilia (pop. 70) is an old village in San Jacinto County. When I was in Camilia the last time I learned that Sarah Thornton had died. She was a former slave. And I'd last talked to her in 1966 at the O. J. Jordan general store in Camilia. At that time she said she was born a slave 106 years before. And Camilia old-timers told me this was true.

She was a sharp-witted brown woman with white hair in short braids framing a smiling face.

"I was born on a plantation owned by the McGowen family here near Camilia. Only I didn't do much slavin'. I was freed when I was a child."

She lived in a little farm on which she said "her poor little husband" worked most of their lives and raised twelve children.

"Work never hurt nobody. I worked in the fields, only I

would come in early and fix supper for those kids and my poor little husband." (Her husband had been dead for several years when I talked with her.)

She said she had been baptized about ninety-five years before in the nearby Trinity River, "and I've been a child of God ever since."

While Mrs. Thornton was enjoying a bottle of red soda pop a salesman came in the store and said: "Hello Auntie."

She replied to this: "I ain't your aunt. Be you a child of God I am your sister."

She figured that I was a preacher, despite my denial that I'd taken holy orders. She kept calling me "preacher man." She said her formula for a long life was "to work hard and love most everyone and eat common foods and try not to get vexed and to be a child of God."

This sweet personality said she had spent all of her life on the little farm near Camilia except for brief visits to Waco and to Houston.

"Preacher man," she said to me, "they's too much fuss in those big towns. Too much fuss. They is really some fuss in that Houston town. I love it here in San Jacinto County where they is pretty fields and big trees and quiet. And I can hear the same church bells my mother and father heard in the long, long ago."

9

May's Cafe in a Cow Pasture

"I was told," said May Martin, "that I was good-looking when I was a young gal and just getting a start here in the cafe business. I can't say for sure, though, because I had a husband who worked me so hard I never got a chance to look for very long in a mirror.

"Well, in that time when I was considered easy on the eyes, a big and mean-drunk young oil field roughneck come in my cafe and was giving my waitress a hard time. Finally, the roughneck come over to me at the counter and said: 'May, I'm going to get in your pants.' Well, I taken off my bloomers and I pulled a six-shooter from under the counter and I said: 'Okay, Mr. Man.' And I made that varmint put on my bloomers and parade around. That taught him a good lesson, and he was polite the next time he come to my place."

In 1983 May Martin had been in the cafe business for fifty-four years. And May's Cafe, in Henderson County, Texas, nine miles south of Athens, has been an institution since the long-ago time when the late billionaire Sid Richardson of Athens was eating there on credit. The small frame restaurant in a cow pasture owned by May Martin causes cars and trucks to be parked for a two-hundred-yard stretch along Highway 19 at noontime seven days a week. May's delicious fare, country-cured ham smoked on the premises and heavy on homegrown vegetables in season, is served only at "dinner," meaning luncheon in rural Texas language.

I like to come to May's when the spring greens from her gardens are simmering in smoked bacon. That's the time when many birds are welcomed back to Mrs. Martin's little livestock farm.

"I got no regular tame pets. But I got a lot of wild pets that I feed and they come calling on me regularly, such as an old bobcat. I got lots of birds, such as cardinals, mockingbirds, crows, quails, and doves. I got dove calls at sunup and sundown and coyote music at night."

In the spring the African cattle egrets return to Henderson County. May will point out a cafe window facing her cow pasture and she will say:

"Looks at them big white boogers out there! Some of them birds are roosting on cows' backs and scratching in the hides for ticks and other clinging insects and some of them are on the ground gobbling bugs stirred up by the cow creatures' hooves. Birds that are friends with cattle! Just beautiful. I think a lot of them big white birds."

I asked May how she got into the cafe business back in 1929. She answered: "Well, I was always considered right smart of a cook. And when I was young I was married up with a farmer man who not only expected me to do the cooking and housekeeping and caring for the children, but also to help him make a crop. Also that husband was bad about wandering off and staying away for a spell. I got tired of this. And my brother gave me some money to go in the cafe business. And here I been, seven days a week."

In the spring in Henderson County, the flowering dogwoods make a brave show against the backdrop of pines and hardwood, and there are many little lakes in the timbered hills.

Once when the dogwoods were in bloom I was headed for the annual "washpot stew" party at Bill Perryman's house on Rainbow Lake, not far from May's Cafe. Before going to the Perryman party, I stopped off to talk with Mrs. Martin.

She pretended to be miffed when I told her I was headed for festivities at the Perrymans', and she said: "Bill and Mary Ann forgot to invite me this spring, and you tell them Perrymans that their credit is cut off at May's."

Mrs. Martin said that Sid Richardson and another Athens billionaire, the late Clint Murchison, Sr., "ran a tab at my place long after they became big rich."

One of May's oldest customers is ninety-three-year-old (in 1983) Edward Broughton Gauntt, a retired Athens merchant who wears preppy clothes and "goes dancing several nights a week with my sweet little widow."

Athens is called "The Black-Eyed Pea Capital of the World" and celebrates each July with a festival which includes a "world championship" black-eyed pea cooking contest. Edward Gauntt says that May Martin is the real champ at cooking black-eyed peas and he raises his own peas in his backyard and cooks them intelligently. Of his friend Mrs. Martin, he said:

"May cooks blackeyes and about everything else the way I do. And that's the right way. Not many cafe cooks can bring out the true flavor of blackeyes. I take friends out to May's Cafe often. Only you got to be careful what you say to May or she may give you a good cussing out. When I come in her cafe, I don't say anything but hello to her until she says something to me. I don't want to get cussed out."

John Deibel, one of the organizers of the black-eyed pea festival, asked Mrs. Martin to help judge the cook-off in 1982. She refused without explanation. So, in company with two television-type journalists, Jack Brown and Jocelyn White of Dallas, I went out to ask Mrs. Martin why she wouldn't help us judge the contest.

She looked at the beautiful Jocelyn and at Jack Brown and said: "If I was a red-mouthed television spieler from Dallas, I wouldn't mind being a pea judge. But I got to live and run a business here in Henderson County. And was I a pea judge, I would make a few friends among the winners and a lot more enemies among the losing cooks."

10

Pap Has Been Plowing
More Than One Hundred Years

Walter Harris doesn't know his exact age. Of one thing he is certain. He has been plowing more than one hundred years.

"Sometime in the 1870s I went to part of one session of a country school called Grand Prairie in Grimes County," he said. "Then I had to quit school for good. That was more than one hundred years ago. And I been plowing ever since."

Walter Harris, known as "Pap," is a tall, slender, broad-shouldered black man. He has a stern countenance and catlike yellow-green eyes. He lives in Celina, Collin County, with his third wife Gertrude, and his lively, eleven-year-old adopted son Frederick Harris.

Harris works for farmers and ranchers around Celina, most often for (and with) an eighty-four-year-old white friend John Willock.

About twenty-three years ago Harris checked to see if he was eligible for social security. Research by the social security people with old-timers in Grimes County (who said that they were young people when he was a grown man) indicated he was about ninety at the time. And that was twenty-three years ago.

"Pap isn't the type to fib about his age," said John Willock. "You can believe what he says. If you could see him climbing over fences and gates and plowing all day and feeding cattle you might think he's a lot younger."

He sometimes speaks up at meetings of the St. Phillip Baptist Church, across the street from his home in Celina. He said he needs a place to "speak his mind. We're living in a heathen world now. Most everyone is aiming at enjoyment and trying to dodge work. Most don't know what a day's hard work is, and the older people who would like to work are put out to pasture in a rest home or hospital. It's a terrible thing to cut off an able-bodied person from work just because he or she happens to hit sixty-five. When a person stays idle the devil has a lot to work with."

Pap speaks well and with no noticeable accent. There are none of the sounds in his speech of a fellow with only a few weeks of formal schooling and more than a century as a field hand. He told me:

"I learned my ABCs from my *Playmate Reader* when I was in school. That's all. I didn't learn to really read until I was about fifty. The first thing I was able to read all the way was the first chapter of the Gospel of St. John. In the last sixty-odd years though I've read books by the thousands."

At the side of his house he has a machine shed where he does repair work on his pickup truck and on lawn mowers. He has one rider mower. He and eleven-year-old Frederick mow lawns when there is no farm work. In fact, on two occasions when I've stopped to talk with this ancient plowman he was riding around the neighborhood mowing lawns for free just to keep busy.

He smokes cigars, and he likes a beer after work. I've never seen him smile, though. I asked him about his characteristic dour expression.

"Well, there's not much to smile about when you're living in a world that's getting more heathen every day," he replied. "Our leaders aren't acting like leaders and most people aren't particular about their lives."

He has had a few health problems in recent years.

"About six years ago my water stopped, and I had to have a prostate operation. That's all right now. I sometimes have kind of blackout spells if I don't keep moving. So I keep moving and plowing when there's plowing to be done."

He sows hundreds of acres of wheat for John Willock and

others, and he works in the harvests, and then he is busy plowing up the wheatlands.

Walter Harris and his three wives (he has been a widower twice since 1895) have had nine children. The oldest is now in his eighties and the youngest is sixty-three.

He adopted Frederick when the child was a month old. Why should a man more than one hundred years old adopt a baby?

"That baby needed a home," he said. "Now that he's eleven, he's real nice company. Having a child in the household keeps you lively."

11

A Rough-Tongued Priest

He was known as San Isidro the Farmer or the Laborer. He died in A.D. 1130. And he was canonized, or so goes the legend, after an angel was seen operating his plow. He is the patron saint of farmers and others who work with their hands.

San Isidro lives again in 1983 in Dell City, Texas, in the brawny person of Father John F. Casey, aged seventy-four.

Dell City (pop. 383) is in Hudspeth County in heavily mineralized earth just west of some salt lakes and the nine thousand-foot-high Guadalupe Mountains. Dell City is the center for a lush farming community which blossomed out of the desert about a quarter of a century ago when it was found to be over an underground lake.

Father Casey is a rough-tongued Boston Irishman, his brogue somewhat softened from many years spent with Spanish-speaking Texas parishioners.

"I took four years of Spanish in high school and one year of it in college. Yet, Castilian Spanish is a waste in my parish. You gotta speak Juarez Spanish. They don't know what the hell you're saying in Castilian," said the padre.

He played football at Boston College and four other colleges. Then he became a carpenter. And he was thirty-two when he entered the priesthood.

The muscular, 190-pound, former football center did all the carpentry work, all the plumbing, all the electrical wiring and the plastering on the two large buildings that comprise San Isidro Catholic Mission.

The original 1955 model church is now a recreation hall and the old priest's living quarters.

His latest triumph is the new church with an auditorium which seats more than five hundred. It would probably cost at least two hundred thousand dollars, maybe more, to construct if you didn't have San Isidro's 1983 disciple on the job.

"I built that church with fifty thousand dollars and twenty pounds off my butt," said Father Casey.

He only had help on the concrete block walls and the roof.

The front of the new church is graced with pictures of the angel at San Isidro's plow, these artworks in brilliant Mexican tiles.

Father Casey once applied for an on-the-premises beer license for San Isidro. He said he needed a beer license to keep his congregation together," said Judge Tom Neely of Sierra Blanca, the capital of Hudspeth County. Judge Neely told me he didn't know how Father Casey came out on his application.

"Actually I sold beer at church dances and suppers until someone turned me in and the liquor control people stopped me," said the padre. "Now my parishioners have to bring their beer. Hell of a note! I never got a beer license."

The feast of San Isidro, around May 10, is always a big day at Father Casey's church. On that date he also blesses the crops.

Several years ago I was in Dell City when Father Casey got a complaint from one of the farmers, Joe Diaz.

"Padre, you bless my crops in May and in June I got some hail damage. What kind of a deal is that?" said Mr. Diaz.

"Hell, Joe, you never go to church. What do you expect?" was Father Casey's reply.

Dell City is rather isolated. It's about seventy miles to the nearest real town, the county seat, Sierra Blanca, and one hundred miles to El Paso.

About a decade ago or more the Dell City citizens petitioned the state to let them form their own political division, called Sam Rayburn County, in honor of the late speaker of the House of Representatives from Texas.

The Dell City citizens' main gripe was that it is seventy lonely miles to the Hudspeth County courthouse.

Nothing came of the petition though. Hudspeth County is almost as big as the state of Connecticut in area but has less than three thousand inhabitants, most of these in and around Sierra Blanca and Dell City.

Sam Rayburn County, if it had been organized, wouldn't have had enough human types to afford a courthouse—unless Father Casey would build it.

12

Bill Willie's Private Jungle

Bill Willie Gilder looks a lot like the professional comedian Redd Foxx, only Mr. Gilder is darker and probably much more lithe. In 1979, Bill Willie was eighty and he lived at the edge of a jungle path near Cypress Creek in Hardin County and also in East Texas' Big Thicket country.

I drove along winding trails in a high forest before I came to a dead end. And there was Bill Willie Gilder's neat white cottage in a little clearing.

"You don't pass my place going anywhere," said Mr. Gilder, speaking of his splendid isolation.

There was dense vegetation round the clearing, one hundred-foot-high sweet gum trees, thickets of privets with cylindrical spikes of white blossoms, sassafras trees heavy with greenish-yellow blooms, and Bill Willie's pride, satsuma mandarin orange trees in tender flower.

And there were swamps, muddy water swamps.

"The water is so thick around here I keep a possum for a yard dog," joked Mr. Gilder.

He said he'd never traveled much except for one journey up in the Midwest and including Chicago.

"I didn't like it up in that Yankee country. Too much bother in places like Chicago. Right now you could go farther around a hambone looking for lean meat than I get out of Hardin County." He has lived all his life in Hardin County. And he is one of the most knowledgeable horticulturists in the Big Thicket. He is much sought after for services such as grafting trees.

His reputation has gone beyond East Texas. Once he was offered a big-money job as a horticulturist in California.

"I told them I'm not going to ever leave this forest. I don't want to live nowhere I can't make a garden and go fishing when I want to."

Although he probably knows more about the lush plant life of the Big Thicket than anyone, Mr. Gilder told me he doesn't actually live in the Thicket.

"Looks like the Tight-eye Thicket to me," I said, speaking of a part of the Big Thicket where you have to strain your eyes sometimes to see a few feet ahead.

"Nope," said the old man. "They's no palmettos in here. See some palmettos and it's a sure sign you in the Big Thicket. The Big Thicket start near here, though." And he pointed in the direction of the nearby town of Kountze.

We'd been sitting on the Gilder cottage's front steps. Low, dark clouds were gathering. "Them are nervous clouds," said Bill Willie. And it began to rain big drops, splashing among the masses of chlorophyll in Mr. Gilder's jungle.

Bill Willie brought out a couple of chairs, one with a cowhide bottom and that intimate look of a handmade thing, for me and one with a deer-hide seat for himself.

He is unique in that he named himself—at least he picked his Christian names. He'd told me how this happened on another visit years before:

"I was the onliest boy in our family. They was nine gals. My mamma and my papa just called me Son—they did until I was old enough to get mighty tired of being called Son. One day I come to the house for Papa was calling for Son. I said: 'Papa, my name's not Son! I'm Bill Willie!' And I been Bill Willie ever since."

A Dr. William Ethridge drove up along the path through the jungle and got out of his pickup truck. He had a dozen or so nectarines in his hand. He said to Mr. Gilder:

"Bill Willie, these nectarines are all off the same tree. And yet as you can see some are very large and some are quite small. There must be more than a thousand nectarines on that tree. But the mystery to me is why some of the fruit is large and some is quite small."

"Well," said the old horticulturist, "I'll have to come and see before I can really tell you. But I'd say that tree has overfruited."

"A lot of people around here depend on you," Dr. Ethridge said to Bill Willie. "And you seem to get along with everyone."

"If I don't like a man I feed him out of a long-handled spoon," Mr. Gilder replied. "And if I really don't like him I tell him I live at the end of the Big Muddy and I got a 30/30." (By "30/30" he meant the caliber of his rifle.)

Bill Willie was getting hoarse voiced. And he told me he hadn't been "feeling peart" lately.

"I know what I need is some sassafras tea and some crackling bread. I got plenty of sassafras but I don't run my own piney woods rooters (hogs) for the cracklings anymore. This country is getting too settled up for a man to have rooters loose in the woods and I got no time for set hogs. (By set hogs he meant those kept in pens.) I used to turn my rooters loose on the mast and chewfers, and then before hog-killing time I'd feed them baits of sweet potatoes to firm up the flesh."

Mr. Gilder had been looking at a book on the Big Thicket in which there was a complimentary story about him and his work as a horticulturist.

"This is a mighty pretty book except they's too much of the word 'nigger' in it. I don't like that word. I once worked for a man who called me darky. But he never dared call me nigger. That's a word you can put on anyone. A man can be as white as a lock of cotton and still be a nigger."

13

The Moonshiner of Drunkard's Branch

I didn't meet Jethro Holmes until his last years when he had retired as Tyler County's most popular producer of moonshine whiskey and, at age eighty-four, had gone into the business of topping tall trees. And there are plenty of very tall trees in Tyler County. The last time I talked with him was at his ancestral tree farm on Drunkard's Branch and near the Piney Woods town of Woodville, Texas. Jethro was cussing the store-bought whiskey he'd had to settle for on Christmas Eve and sampling it cautiously.

"Damned stuff tastes like it's got fusel oil in it," he complained. "There was never such in whiskey of my making. For more than sixty years I made the purest moonshine whiskey and peach brandy a person ever poured down his or her'n gullet. No sting. And no fusel oil to cause a hangover."

Just before I crossed the small, clear stream called Drunkard's Branch there was a sign which read: "J. H. Holmes, tree expert." Even when he was well along in his eighties the old man had an apelike agility in trees and a good understanding of them and he thought nothing of topping the tallest timber in East Texas.

On the Christmas Eve I visited with him last, Jethro was also cussing the weather. Every year he played Santa Claus for the children of Woodville and Tyler County, although he needed lots of padding for the role. He would arrive in downtown Woodville on Christmas Eve in a wagon made up to look like a sleigh pulled by two giant oxen called Tom and Jerry. (In his old age he continued to make artistic oxen yokes and he used Tom and Jerry and the wagon for transport between Drunkard's Branch and town.) He had the sleigh loaded with gifts and he would take the children on rides in it.

"Soon as this damned rain stops and all the bullfrog music we been having stops I'm going to hitch Tom and Jerry to the wagon and take the rig to the Woodville schools and show them little scholars how we got around in the olden days. Oxen broke the first ground in these parts and them creatures is still handy for pulling stuff in the baygalls and marshes where a tractor will get mired," said Jethro.

He served one hitch in prison for making illegal whiskey, and it is said that the judge, who sentenced him reluctantly, was a long-time customer.

"When I come back to Woodville after being gone eleven months all my customers met me at the bus station with a band of music," said Holmes. "They was sure glad to get me back and making whiskey and peach brandy. I was supposed to stay in the pen for nine months. Only I'm right smart of an engineer and they put me to building a two hundred thousand-dollar hog house for the prison. I stayed on an extra two months to finish the hog house. I always aim to finish anything I start."

That Christmas Eve on Drunkard's Branch Jethro risked another snort of the store-bought Bourbon. Then he took a chain saw and went out in the tall pines around his house to get a Christmas tree. In the old tradition, the Holmes family doesn't raise the yule tree until Christmas Eve.

Jethro said he had months of severe combat duty in France while in the Army in World War I. "I was in Brest, France, getting ready to leave for home on Christmas Eve, 1918, and I taken six of my men (he was a sergeant) out in the woods and cut down a Christmas tree. We set it up in Woodrow Wilson Square in Brest and fitted it out with red, white, and blue pretties."

He said he had a French girl friend and her family owned a small brandy distillery.

"That girl was mighty sweet on me. She wanted me to marry up with her and help run the distillery. Like a fool I didn't take her up on it. If I'd stayed in France I could have made all the brandy I wanted without the high sheriff and the federal men pestering me. For years during Prohibition I moved around like a coyote, sometimes making my moonshine in Tyler County and sometimes in Hardin and Jasper counties. That old judge, who later sentenced me, was a big customer of mine, as I told you. Every time district court met here in Woodville I would supply one hundred gallons of rye whiskey and brandy for the judge and his staff so they could show how friendly and hospitable our town was. That old judge still had a lot of years staked out ahead of him when he was drinking my whiskey like a hog. The only trouble with drinking as I see it is that the gossips will wait until you finally die and say whiskey done it."

Jethro said that his family had been making moonshine whiskey in East Texas since the 1836–1846 days of the Republic of Texas. And one of his inheritances was a "double thumper" copper still.

"I guess you'd say I become a moonshiner when I was only seven or eight years old and a scholar in the *Second Reader* at the Drunkard's Branch schoolhouse. My papa would fire up the still and leave me to cook up nine or ten gallons of rye whiskey so pure and soft you could drink it like soda pop. We needed about that much each week for family use and to give friends and to pay off hoe hands.

"We didn't sell no whiskey but when times was tough and money was dear whiskey could be used to pay hoe hands."

The last time I talked with the old moonshiner was during the "swine influenza" epidemic of the late 1970s. He told me: "I don't feel peart. They say I got that cussed pig flu."

A month or so later I was in Woodville and planned to go out and visit my friend on Drunkard's Branch. Only the clerk at the Dogwood Inn Motel told me that Jethro had died.

THE
GOOD OLD BOYS

14

Lady Bird's Father

The one hundred ten square miles of watery jungles called
Caddo Lake is in both Texas and Louisiana. In the old days
and in some rare cases today, this lake, masked in moss-hung
trees that grow in the water, was a favored haunt for makers
of moonshine whiskey.

The price in Prohibition times for Caddo Lake whiskey was
two to three dollars a gallon. The illicit distillers usually had
copper stills and took pride in their product.

A pair of old Caddo Lake boatmen, Wyatt Moore and
Shinola Hale, told me about the time when almost all of the
Caddo Lake moonshiners (except for Mr. Hale and Mr.
Moore) were rounded up and put in jail in the town of Jeffer-
son, the seat of Marion County and on a bayou leading down
to the lake.

Now making good drinking whiskey was just a sideline for
most of the moonshiners. They were also hardworking
farmers. Some were tenants on the vast croplands of T. J.
(Cap) Taylor, father of Mrs. Lady Bird Johnson.

"Mister Taylor was a good old man," said Shinola Hale.
"Cap would do almost anything for you except let you get out
of debt to his store in Karnack called T. J. Taylor, Dealer in
Everything."

"Cap kindly practiced socialism in a way, although the old
sockwad would have been mad if he heard me say this," said
Wyatt Moore. "Anyway, he charged high prices for those who
could afford to pay and he carried the poor ones if they didn't
try his patience too much."

Shinola didn't like Wyatt's interruption. He wanted to get on with his story about the moonshiners: "Cap Taylor was mighty alarmed when he heard that his best farmers was in jail over to Jefferson. For it was harvest time. Cap said in his whiny, high voice: 'Something has got to be did. I got to get them boys out of the jailhouse or the crops will spoil. Them that makes the best drinking whiskey is also the best farmers.'

"So he went over to the Jefferson courthouse and seen the judge.

"Cap always looked like he'd just come in on a freight train. He was a kindly medium-sized, biscuit-bodied man. He liked to go barefooted in warm weather except when the cockleburs was mature. Now they was a young newcomer judge working the court at Jefferson who didn't know that Cap was Mister Boss, the biggest landowner in two counties.

"When the judge come in court Cap didn't stand up but just sat there in his straw hat and overalls. And he got bawled out by the judge good.

"Cap taken off his hat, stood up, and stated his business, saying he wanted to bail out all of the moonshiners, and he said he wished it weren't no crime to make good drinking whiskey. He also stated that they couldn't make a harvest until the men got out of jail.

"Well, the newcomer judge gave Cap a mean look and he said: 'Old man, you got any land to put up for surety?' Cap whined: 'I got a little bit, Judge!' The judge kept after him: 'How much you got?' And Cap studied for a spell and whined: 'Maybe thirty-five thousand acres, Judge.'

"Well, the boys was let out of jail. And the crops was laid by. And the antimoonshine sentiment slacked off. And the boys didn't face no charges. And after things had blowed over we all went back to making whiskey in our spare time."

Shinola Hale lived for all of his seventy-eight years on Caddo Lake. Up until 1980 he was the "mayor" of Whiskey Point, a terminal of Pine Island. There he had boats for rent and he was a guide—you don't go out in Caddo's mazes and mysteries, unless you've been there for a long time, without a guide. Wyatt Moore has it on his business card that he is a "Caddo Lake and river pilot."

Shinola's bait shop is a more than century-old building said to have once been on the main street of a ghost town on the lake called Port Caddo. At the time he was talking with Wyatt and me, Shinola was carrying an old double-barreled shotgun. He said he'd been out in the lake running his traps and the shotgun was used to shoot tree-climbing water snakes.

"Something has got to be did about a preacher for our church house or we won't have no church house soon here on Whiskey Point," said Shinola.

By church house Shinola meant a picturesque frame building on stilts at the lake's edge and partly in the lake during high water. This building, with steeple and bell tower, was raised sometime in the 1970s for a set in several Disney motion pictures about the Louisiana bayous—the Texas shore of Caddo Lake looks more like most folks' idea of Louisiana than the Louisiana side of the lake does.

"Them movie-making people said we could have this church house as soon as they was done with it," said Shinola. "All we need now is a preacher who is not too lazy to do some work on the church house. If he likes to fish, a preacher would be happy here."

"Quit changing the subject. We're talking about Cap Taylor," said Wyatt Moore. "He come here in 1898 or '99. He said he brought five hundred dollars with him. He said he was going to go back to Alabama, where he was from, and fetch his sweetheart to get married—as soon as he got rich in Texas.

"It didn't really take him long, at that, to get right smart property in and around Karnack.

"He bought sixteen acres of land across the road from the Karnack cotton gin. And he put in a little store in which he claimed he sold everything from sardines to plow points, although he really didn't have much stock at first. Cap put in a

crop on his sixteen acres. And when he was busy with his plot
of land and a customer come up for his store, he would just
hand the customer the key and let him help himself and then
come back where he was plowing and return the key and make
the payment. Mister Taylor was a great one for trusting
people.

"Next thing you know he took to buying fish caught in
Caddo Lake, catfish and white perch and other kinds, by the
hundreds of pounds. Then he would sell the fish in the big
towns around here."

Vivian Hackney, a retired bank president in Jefferson and
one of the real authorities on the Caddo Lake country mysteries, told me something about Lady Bird's father that not even
his cronies, Wyatt Moore and Shinola Hale, knew.

"Vivian Hackney told me that Cap Taylor made a lot of
money in caviar," I told the two old boatmen. "Actually it was
eggs from Caddo Lake catfish. But he shipped it to the Fulton
Street Fish Market in New York City. And Cap understood it
was sold up there for caviar."

Wyatt said: "I didn't know about this caviar. Cap Taylor
made thousands of dollars selling fish. But I never saw him fish
himself but one time. And that was when he came up to our
moonshining camp here on the lake right smack on the Texas-
Louisiana border. It was handy then having our camps on the
boundary line between the two states. For a moonshiner could
jump sideways and be in another state in case of trouble in the
state he'd been standing on before."

It must have been a very pleasant camp as Wyatt described
it. The cooking was done by a real chef, Sachihiko (Ona)
Murata, a Japanese pearl fisherman. Then there was Frank
Galbraith, Sr., the best boatbuilder on Caddo Lake. (Wyatt
Moore now claims that distinction and he has built big craft
for carrying oil field equipment. He has one vessel which is a
dead ringer for *The African Queen* in the Bogart movie. And
he made cyprus boats and Cajun-style canoes for the Disney
movies.)

Another personality who hung around the Moore-Murata-Galbraith camp in those days was one Bush Jarrott, the state hangman of Louisiana.

"Bush Jarrott seemed to spend most of his time between hangings in our camp," said Wyatt. "He fished some. And he brooded. You could tell the hangings were telling on old Bush for he drank more than his share of our good moonshine whiskey. He was a nice man."

Shinola said that Ona Murata came to Caddo Lake as an oil field cook. Before that he had been an enlisted cook in the U. S. Navy.

Wyatt went on: "Ona could make delicious dishes with catfish and gaspar goo [gaspergou]. No one could cook rice more beautifully than that little Japanese. And his chicken curry was something to remember.

When World War II came along some of the authorities wanted to put the old Japanese pearl fisherman in a concentration camp. Only Cap Taylor put a stop to that, probably with help from his son-in-law, Congressman Lyndon Johnson.

On the north side of Caddo Lake there are high bluffs. And Sachihiko Murata is buried on one of those rises over Caddo. He died in 1946 at age eighty-six, and his friend of the moonshiners' camp, Frank Galbraith, Sr., is buried nearby with a legend on his gravestone which reads: "Builder of Fine Boats."

T. J. Taylor told me he took his bride, the former Minnie Patillo, from his home country in Alabama to their new Texas home in 1904. It was called The Brick House. It and Douglas Blocker's grand seigneur mansion nearby, Mimosa Hall, were the most splendid dwellings in the Caddo Lake countryside, when they were built in 1843–1844.

John J. Webster, the builder of both The Brick House and Mimosa Hall, was an architect and contractor from Alabama. And he had constructed some of the original buildings of the University of Alabama. Webster brought with him to what was then the Republic of Texas a team of skilled artisans under the direction of a British stonemason, a Mr. Willey, Christian name lost to the records. Mrs. Willey was governess for the Webster children.

The Webster family moved into Mimosa Hall, and a Major Andrews was the first owner of The Brick House.

According to Tony Taylor, T.J.'s son, his father bought the house from a medical doctor with a local reputation for eccentricity.

The old doctor collected hickory nuts. Boy, did he collect hickory nuts! One bedroom was almost completely filled with hickory nuts when the Taylors moved into The Brick House in 1904.

15

Old Man Garner

One time in Uvalde I was watching baseball on television with John Garner. At about one o'clock the heady aroma of Mexican food was coming from the kitchen. Garner's cook came in the den and asked me:

"Are you going to stay and have lunch with Old Man Garner?"

I said yes, of course.

Then when the cook had gone back in the kitchen I asked the thirty-second Vice President of the United States:

"Didn't that woman offend you, calling you Old Man Garner?"

"Goddamn it!" replied Mr. Garner. "I am eighty-five years old. I AM Old Man Garner. Of course, that woman could have no cause for complaint if I took a notion to call her Fatso. Only I wouldn't say anything like that to a woman, especially if she is a damned good cook. Let's go eat some Mexican food."

From the middle 1950s to the mid-'60s, I went out of my way to stop in Uvalde and visit with John Garner. He was such a classic curmudgeon that he fascinated me. And when he spoke there was often wisdom in the expressions of his cantankerous humor.

If Mance Lipscomb had known him he would have said: "Here is a man with a good Mojo Hand!" For Mr. Garner had a lot of good things happen to him during his long life. He was born on November 22, 1868. And he died in Uvalde in 1967, fifteen days shy of his 99th birthday.

When he was bidding for the presidency, after serving two terms as Vice President in the Franklin Roosevelt administration, he claimed that he was born in a log cabin "in Red River County, Texas, about thirty miles from Indian Territory."

One time to get the old boy's blood circulating I told him I doubted that story about him being born in a log cabin. "Your papa was a prosperous saloonkeeper in Detroit, Texas, and how many wealthy saloonkeepers let their children be born in a log cabin?"

I was kidding him. His father was a saloonkeeper, but I doubted if he was wealthy.

Mr. Garner said he was quite familiar with farkleberry trees, although not with the mystique connected with the farkle. When he was a young man back in Red River County he played on the Coon Soup Hollow ball team. And he carved a farkleberry limb into the likeness of a baseball bat. For, he said, the Coon Soup Hollow team had to scratch around for equipment.

"I dearly love baseball, and I went to as many games as I could when I was in Washington," he said. "At least two fellows who wrote books about me put it down that I was a baseball player during my early days in East Texas. The truth is that with the Coon Soup Hollow team we just played what we called 'town ball,' a crude form of baseball. We had a hard rubber ball and a farkle stick or some other kind of homemade bat. In those days I was right smart of a hitter. And I could run like a scalded dog."

He was known as Cactus Jack in Washington. He got that nickname when he was a youthful member of the Texas legislature from Uvalde and he was trying to get the prickly pear bloom named the official Texas state flower.

However, a successful lobby by women of the state caused the legislature to make the bluebonnet the state flower.

Now most ranchers consider the bluebonnet a bad weed mainly because cows won't eat it.

"Goddamned stinkweed," said Garner. "Something that doesn't taste sweet in the mouth of a cow shouldn't be the state flower."

Even in his old age (or until his last two helpless years) Mr. Garner was a formidable personality. He had the look of a bold old owl with his beaked nose and heavy white eyebrows and his narrow hooded eyes.

I put up with a lot of his rudeness.

For instance, once when I was passing the time of day with him in the sunshine on the lawn of his home some visitors came by and Garner introduced me this way:

"I'm being pestered by this goddamned snoop from the Dallas *News*. He mooches my cigars and drinks my whiskey and stays for dinner when there's Mexican food."

He didn't mean what he said. Unlike many curmudgeons he had his humble side. When he was in his nineties he told me: "I guess some folks who come to Uvalde to see the former vice president of the United States expect to see a big, imposing man. And all they see is me, a little old runt of a Democrat."

Mr. Garner was what he called "a kiss bug." He explained: "If they don't object too much, I like to kiss women visitors hello and when they're ready to leave I like to kiss them good-bye."

This happened most often when he was sitting in the sunshine of his lawn. When he saw some women coming he would always put out the ashes of his cigar, wrap the cigar in a handkerchief and stow it for future smoking in a breast pocket of his coat.

"For an old sockwad like me chances for kissing a girl are mighty poor if I'm puffing like a teakettle on a cigar," he explained.

Once I was there just as some women were leaving the

lawn, probably after being kissed. Mr. Garner took the wrapped-in-a-handkerchief cigar from his pocket, and after he examined it he yelled: "Goddamn it! I broke the end off my cigar while I was playing the kiss bug and bowing and scraping for those girls."

.

It happened that I attended the big day in Mr. Garner's life, his ninetieth birthday. Former President Harry Truman, Speaker of the House Sam Rayburn, U. S. senators Ralph Yarborough and Lyndon Johnson were among the guests of a big party hosted by a future Texas governor, Dolph Briscoe.

Mr. Garner gave more than a million dollars to improve Southwest Texas Junior College in Uvalde, and he was a very charitable person. However, he was tightfisted with money sometimes—in fact most of the time.

He hadn't bought any clothes since he left Washington in 1941. And his son Tully wanted him to buy a new sombrero and a new suit for his ninetieth birthday. After he priced these articles of clothing in local stores the old man said, "Clothes have become too dear. I'll get along with my old things."

Finally Tully Garner figured out how to back his father into a new suit. He went to a department store and made a one-hundred-dollar down payment and told the clothier that he would talk his father into returning to the store and any suits he tried on should be priced one hundred dollars less than the listed price.

While he listened to speeches praising him by Harry Truman, Lyndon Johnson, and the others, Mr. Garner wore his new Stetson without any creases.

"Your hat looks like a hen's nest," Tully told him.

"You put creases in a felt hat and it'll wear out quickly in the creases," said this multimillionaire. "I never crease a felt hat."

He was a good ranch-style cook. On hunting trips he would sometimes serve as the cook—this until he was about seventy-five. And even with a Dutch oven on the trail he could make complex dishes such as wild grape pie.

The high trees around his home were the nesting places for hundreds of white-winged doves. He had great affection for these big birds—at least they are big for doves.

"I like dove calls of an evening," he said. "My doves fly fifteen miles and back every day and bring seeds from croplands and berries from the hill country for their babies."

He seemed quite positive about the doves' daily mileage in the air during the nesting season.

He told me several times during times when the whitewings were nesting: "I'm going to shoot some goddamned cats if they don't quit stalking my doves and their babies." He spoke the last words fiercely, and then in a quieter tone he added:

"I like dove calls. And frog bells."

He had a good marriage although his courtship of Miss Mariette Rheiner of Uvalde didn't start until after they had been political opponents. They were both candidates for Uvalde County judge. Mr. Garner won after a rough campaign. They were married a few months later.

After Mrs. Garner died in 1950, Mr. Garner moved out of their mansion and into a small cottage in the backyard. And he gave the big house to Uvalde for a public library.

For twenty years after he left Washington, John Garner still had a lot of influence on Texas voters. U. S. Senator Yarborough wrote: "Garner's famed 'quail breakfast' for Harry Truman at Uvalde on Truman's lonesome campaign trail in 1948 gave Truman a boost that ballooned into enormous crowds throughout Texas and helped elect Truman for his second term. Garner supported Adlai Stevenson with a similar breakfast in Uvalde in 1952, and he gave hearty endorsements for John Kennedy in 1960 and Lyndon Johnson in 1964."

From 1941 when he left Washington until 1961 Garner's only motorcar was a 1940 Ford sedan.

In 1961, with some help from one of his longtime Uvalde

friends, Lucas Zamoro, Mr. Garner swapped the "old, smooth-mouthed Ford" for a 1951 International pickup. Since both Mr. Garner and Mr. Zamoro were rough dressers unless company was coming, they looked like two poverty-stricken types tooling around in that rusty old truck, with Zamoro at the wheel.

One afternoon on the lawn when he was cussing tomcats for preying on his beloved white-winged doves, I tried to steer him into denouncing some prominent Republicans. I knew I couldn't get any adverse criticisms of Democrats from the old loyalist.

"I quit politics in 1941, and that includes talking about it," he replied. "Anyway, if I was to say something bad about one of them big, fat Republicans he might come down here and whip me."

16

John Neely Bryan,
the Wild Indians' Friend Who Founded Dallas

The career of John Neely Bryan has not been well documented in previous histories. He was the strange frontier lawyer who, in a sworn but typically evasive statement, said he founded the town of Dallas "previous to 1840." When I was uncovering some fresh evidence of his fascinating saga, one of the first straightforward comments I found made for the record was that he studied law mainly so he could help his Indian friends in their dealings with white folks.

In the past most accounts of earliest Dallas happenings make John Neely Bryan a kind of dog-eared version of the Lone Ranger, complete with a faithful, Tonto-like Indian companion named Ned. And the man who founded Dallas in a wilderness is astride a saddle horse with a poetic Indian name said to translate as Walking Wolf.

The Indian, Ned, then vanishes from what Hubert Mewhinney once called "the fable of Dallas' founding." Mewhinney (pronounced "mee-WHEE-knee" with a horsey accent) was a Houston *Post* columnist who enjoyed baiting the city of Dallas.

He once asked me about Bryan's Indian friend: "Who the hell was Ned? He makes only one guest appearance in Dallas' fable. I'll bet you can't prove that Ned really existed!"

I can't be sure but there is strong evidence that John Neely Bryan's aboriginal friend at the start of Dallas was a shrewd Delaware chief and dealer in hides and bear fat, Jim Ned.

He had to be a friend of Bryan's or his band of Delawares wouldn't have been camped in the Trinity River bottoms near the founder's settlement as early as 1842, according to written record, and perhaps two years earlier. One of the boys in the William Hord family on Hord's Ridge (Oak Cliff) was standing on a high ridge over the Trinity and about to take a shot at Jim Ned's peaceful tribesmen when he was restrained.

Like Bryan the Delaware chief sometimes served as scout or guide for representatives of the Republic of Texas government on hazardous excursions into western Texas to meet with wild Plains Indians, such as the Comanches. (I've wondered why one of the Dallas historians who knew Bryan used only a few sentences to describe what must have been high adventures, saying that "this great-hearted frontiersman" served several times as "Sam Houston's ambassador" to the wild Comanches and Kiowas.)

However, the early Dallas historians must have had bad times trying to interview Bryan, for the founder of Dallas was very secretive about his private life. He never, for the record, revealed "the friend" for whom he named Dallas town. And I've found fresh evidence that the town had its present name in early 1842. This is in a document of one of Bryan's land sales.

I think that previous historians of early Dallas have failed to accent the fact that Bryan's Dallas never suffered from hostile Indians, even when it was a very vulnerable outpost of what passed for civilization in the Republic of Texas era, 1836–1846. Bryan's presence was, of course, the reason Dallas was such a haven. As his widow, Margaret Beeman Bryan, said in an interview with a Burkburnett weekly newspaper, the *Star:* "My husband was a friend of all Indians and he spoke six or seven kinds of Indian talk."

From research I've done I believe that he worked as far away from Dallas as Fort Bridger, the Indian trading post on the Oregon Trail in what is now Wyoming, operated by Jim Bridger, King of the Mountain Men and the discoverer of the Great Salt Lake. And it is certain that he was on the staff of the trading post of Jesse Chisholm, the Cherokee Indian for whom the cattle trail was named, in the "Creek Indian Nation," now Oklahoma, and at Holland Coffee's 1830s Indian trading post on the Red River.

Bryan was very good at covering the tracks of his career. Yet you can get clues from people he claimed as friends in a range from Buffalo Hump, a Comanche war chief, and George Gist or Sequoya, the great Cherokee intellectual, to Sam Houston, President of the Republic of Texas.

It has been written many times that Dallas as a settlement lacked natural advantages and became a great city mostly because of the zeal and industry of its inhabitants. Well, "previous to 1840" when Bryan swore he arrived, the deserted scene that became downtown Dallas certainly had some natural advantages for Republic of Texas wagon and horseback and foot traffic. Bryan filed for his 640 acres on the best low-water gravel ford for miles along those shores. Downstream, as you can see even today, the river was lost for many miles in jungles of trees and sticky, insect- and varmint-ridden underbrush and the banks were high. Upstream there were the three forks of the Trinity to contend with and bayous such as Turtle Creek.

Planners of the Central Highway of the Republic of Texas saw the advantages and came from San Antonio and Austin over a succession of high ridges to Bryan's Ford, by way of the Hord's Ridge (Oak Cliff) highlands and such elevations as the Pisgah Ridge in what are now Limestone, Freestone, and Navarro counties.

For all of wagon train days, even after the Republic of Texas had folded, this was the most traveled trail from Austin and San Antonio by way of Dallas to the Red River.

On the Pisgah Ridge, for example, it was possible to take a wagon or ride horseback from the Brazos River to the Trinity almost on a straight line and encounter little mud even during rainy seasons. Also there were springs of water among the virile, limestone-rooted timber that still flowed even during times of drouth. Even the black mud of the Richland Creek bottom (south of present-day Corsicana) is only three hundred yards wide where the Pisgah Ridge road crossed it, and the main ford of the creek has a rock bottom. Also to the south, the ridge led to the Falls of the Brazos, the only rock-bottomed ford on that stream between the present site of Whitney Dam and the Gulf of Mexico.

From Bryan's Ford at Dallas the Central National Road of the Republic ran to what was then called Travis Wright's Landing, now the village of Kiomatia on the Red River and, later in 1844, the road went to the head of navigation just upstream from Jonesboro in present-day Red River County. This was in a northeasterly direction across what are now Rockwall, Hunt, and Fannin counties.

Also from Bryan's Ford the Preston Road ran almost due north to the Preston Bend of the Red River west of Denison, Texas, and near the village of Fink. Preston Bend and Fort Preston were named for a character even more mysterious than John Neely Bryan, a Lt. William Preston. He was a Republic of Texas second lieutenant and I've not been able to find mention of him in any of the Republic's archives or in the Texas Indians' papers. And yet myriads of landmarks in the Dallas area are named for the second lieutenant of the early 1840s including streets, a bank, golf courses, shopping centers.

In 1982 Dallas land speculators and "developers," many from foreign countries and from other states, were paying billions of dollars for building sites on John Neely Bryan's old square mile of land by the river. They were demolishing landmark buildings until at times downtown looked as if it had gone through a bombing raid. And the speculators were raising new high-rise, high-rent towers.

As early as 1841 greedy land developers from England and the United States got a grant called the Peters Colony and tried to steal Bryan's 640 acres (sometimes listed as 620 acres) by the strategic ford of the Trinity and on the main highway of the Republic.

In 1841 the Republic of Texas government, suffering from weak cash flow, was careless with its grants of public lands. In that year it promised the British-American land speculators, sometimes called the Texas Emigrants and Land Co., thousands of square miles of fertile and mostly unoccupied land in North Texas. On its so-called Peters Colony the group, headed by a family of British musicians who had moved to the United States, was supposed to settle emigrants on millions of acres of land. (One of the Peters clan made a lot of money buying the music compositions of Stephen Foster, such as "Oh! Susannah!," and peddling them for immense profits.)

Unfortunately the 1841 government gave no consideration to the few settlers, including John Neely Bryan, who had already filed claims for acreage within the Peters Colony grant.

The head man of the company was William Smalling Peters, known as "Old Man Peters," and his arrogant British agent-in-charge in Texas was one Henry Oliver Hedgecoxe. They had or assumed the authority to select and locate settlers, where they chose to put them. This included the ones who were already in residence in 1841. Early in that same year Old Man Peters' son-in-law, Samuel Browning, also a colony agent, had given Bryan a certificate for 640 acres but it didn't specify that the land was on the highway by the ford of the Trinity.

Anyway, for fourteen years after he had founded the town in the wilderness, Bryan wasn't able to establish a clear title or patent to what is now downtown Dallas because of interference by the Peters Colony people, especially Hedgecoxe.

John Neely Bryan was born in Fayetteville, Tennessee, on December 24, 1810. Judging by his letters he was well educated for his time, considering he spent most of his life on the frontier. He became a lawyer by studying in the offices of lawyers and by passing the Tennessee bar. But even as a teenager, he was given to running away from home to live with Indians in Tennessee and Arkansas.

There's no precise chronology on when he went off to work in Indian trading posts, those of Holland Coffee at Coffee Station on the Red River and Jesse Chisholm among the Creek Indians in what is now Oklahoma and Jim Bridger at Fort Bridger in Wyoming.

Walter Campbell, usually under the byline of Stanley Vestal, wrote a number of books on the Old West, including the definitive biography of Jim Bridger. Campbell said that John Neely Bryan was "the mystery man of frontier chronicles." Campbell said that he found while working on the Bridger book that Bryan was asked in August 1851, to go to Fort Laramie in what is now Wyoming and act as interpreter at a meeting between U.S. representatives and some of the northern Plains Indians, including the Sioux. Jim Bridger couldn't perform the interpreting chores because his latest Indian wife, Little Fawn, was a Shoshone and the Shoshone were enemies of the Sioux. Campbell didn't find out whether or not Bryan actually showed up at Fort Laramie. But since it happened in the late summer of 1851 it may explain why the Dallas founder wasn't mentioned in the "Hedgecoxe War" in July of that year although he certainly had a grievance against the officious British land agent.

According to the Beeman family Bible, Bryan's wife, Margaret, was born on September 29, 1825, and she died on a September day ninety-four years later in Wichita County, Texas. The Beeman Bible, now in the Hall of State in Dallas' Fair Park, doesn't record it, but Margaret is said to have been born in Calhoun County, Illinois. The John Beeman family in 1840 came from Illinois to Old Boston in Bowie County, Texas. In June 1840, Bryan visited them in Bowie County, or so one Dallas history claims. And, according to the same historian's timetable and an interview with Mrs. Bryan when she was about seventy, the Beeman family moved into the Dallas area near White Rock Creek in June, 1842.

Margaret said in that interview: "My father (John Beeman) and our family came to Dallas in 1842 and I was married in 1843." The marriage, recorded in the Beeman Bible, took place on February 26, 1843. According to most reports the scene for the wedding was Fort Bonham (now Bonham, Texas), about seventy miles to the northeast, or it may have been in the Fannin County seat at the time, Fort Warren. The wedding was held in Fannin County because at the time there was no one in Dallas authorized to perform even a simple civil service.

The life of Margaret and "Neely" (as she always called him) was a happy one for many years, or until Dallas became too civilized for Bryan's taste. Edward Parkinson, a young Englishman, wrote of a visit he made with Sam Houston to Dallas in July 1843. He said the party spent two nights in "a settler's cabin on the river the site for a projected town called Dallas inhabited by a Colonel Bryan, a hardy backwoodsman, sensible, industrious, ingenious and hospitable."

Judging by the Englishman's report, it is no wonder Margaret was so pleased with her husband in the early 1840s. (Incidentally, Parkinson wrote that the rich prairie grasses and the wooded creek bottoms in and around Dallas reminded him of Surrey in England.)

In that newspaper interview when she was in her seventies, Mrs. Bryan said: "We lived happily in that lonely log cabin. We had buffalo, deer and wild turkey for meats and wild honey for sweets. We raised corn on the ground where your fine courthouse now stands and ground it in a little steel mill. Neely had a wooden plow made of a fork of a bois d'arc tree and harness made of buffalo skins, the plow pulled by an Indian pony. We crossed the river in our little canoe dug out of a cottonwood tree. Our first child was born July 17, 1844, and named Holland Coffee Bryan for one of my husband's friends, a trader with the Indians."

You can find out who were some of the mystery man's friends by other names he gave his children: Edward Tarrant for the frontier general for whom Tarrant County was named; Pinckney perhaps for Pinckney Henderson, namesake of Henderson County and once Republic of Texas ambassador to Great Britain and France; Alexander for Alexander Cockrell, the first real industrialist in Dallas who bought what was left of Bryan's headright in 1852.

I've never read any comments by their contemporaries on the physical appearance of the founder and the first lady of Dallas. When he was young Bryan had to be a physical prodigy to make lonely trips in wild country such as journeys to California and back alone. In one photograph made when at least she was youthful in appearance, Margaret is big-eyed and seems a little bewildered. He looks grim and determined, an Indian-like countenance. She has on dark clothing with a white collar. Her hands are held forward, displaying a banded ring on one finger. She has good regular facial features and her hair is up in a dark, severe, middle-parted arrangement. They seem to have a blanket covering their knees, and they are sitting very closely together. He wears a dark coat and what appears to be starchy white linen with a string tie. With white cuffs showing from a coat sleeve, he has one hand on five or six books, perhaps lawbooks, for he brought these from Tennessee when he went to work in the Indian trading posts.

Mrs. Bryan spent the last of her ninety-four years on the farm of one of her sons, John Neely Bryan, Jr., near the village of Charlie and not far from the Red River in Wichita County. She said in an interview with the Burkburnett weekly newspaper that she was glad her son's farm was near the Red River for she could cross over into the Comanche reservation and visit Indian friends there.

My father, H. G. Tolbert, in 1919 was a young oilman drilling wells in and near Burkburnett in Wichita County, and he was present at a reunion of old pioneers and Indians which Margaret Bryan attended. The old lady was asked the cliché question: "I guess the Indians weren't so friendly when you and Mr. Bryan were living on the wild frontier in the early 1840s."

She replied: "From what I hear it's a heap more dangerous to live in Dallas now than it was when I was an eighteen-year-old bride. Neely was good friends with all Indians, even the most ornery of them, and he spoke Indian talk. Dallas was the onliest out-of-way settlement in them early times that wasn't pestered by Indians. That's one reason the land speculators of Peters Colony coveted our lands by the ford."

I have found correspondence between the Bryans in Wichita County and their lawyers in Dallas in which they claimed they still owned the Dallas County courthouse grounds. In the archives of the Dallas County courthouse in 1982 the county's main claim to these grounds is a document in which it is stated that the Bryans were supposed eventually to receive "the penal (?) sum of $5,000" if they "deliver the property to the chief justice of the commissioners court as soon as the patent (title) from the State of Texas is received and provided the seat of justice of Dallas County shall be permanently located in the town of Dallas."

This was filed by Alexander Harwood, county clerk, on October 31, 1850, and "by me (Harwood) recorded this 6th of November, 1850, at 10:20 o'clock P.M." (The man for whom Harwood Street was named must have been working late on that November 6.)

Since the Bryans hadn't received a title to their downtown property in 1850, it may be that the county simply forgot about its promise. There's no record in the Dallas County archives to show that the county actually paid the Bryans $5,000, a hefty sum in those days.

From 1919 until about 1924 according to letters from the Bryans in Wichita County to their representatives in Dallas, they were asking "$2,500 for the property known as the Dallas County public or courthouse square." Could it have been that when Bryan finally got a title to downtown Dallas that the county paid him only $2,500 and reneged on the final $2,500? And that's why the family was demanding $2,500. Anyway, they got nothing unless it was a secret payoff.

Bryan's anxiety over not getting a true title to downtown Dallas for all of the 1840s didn't keep him from giving away town lots to newly married couples and from selling some of the acreage. He also sold some lots.

Morris Britton, M.D., of Sherman, Texas, on January 6, 1981, sent me a copy of an 1842 transaction in which Bryan sold a town lot to one Isaac Young. Dr. Britton wrote to me:

"Recently in Bonham, Texas, I ran across a transaction in Fannin County deeds dated August 27, 1842, which may have been the first recorded use of Dallas as the name for Bryan's new town." Bryan went to Old Warren or Fort Warren, in 1842 the county seat of Fannin County, to file the fact that "I, John Neely Bryan of Dallas, Nacogdoches County, Texas, am bound to Isaac Young of the same place in the penal sum of fifty dollars current money of the Republic of Texas for which payment well and truly be made . . . sealed and dated this 27th day of August, 1842. The condition of this obligation is such that whereas the said John N. Bryan has laid out a town on the east side of the Trinity River which he calls Dallas and whereas the said Isaac Young has purchased John N. Bryan lot No. 6 in block No. 2 on Main Street, being 80 feet front and 160 feet back by reference to the plat of said town made by Lawrence W. Fern, and whereas Isaac Young has this day paid to the above founder of Dallas, J. N. Bryan, the sum of $25."

Bryan was to get the other $25 as soon as he made Young "a good and sufficient deed for the above described lot as soon as Bryan shall obtain a patent for said land . . ."

This hints that the Bryans may have been paid half of the $5,000 for the courthouse grounds but never received the final $2,500 after they got title in 1852. And so they were still seeking the final payment at the time of Mrs. Bryan's death in 1919, and for years after that.

Dr. Britton's 1981 letter on that 1842 transaction mentioned that while Dallas was then a part of Nacogdoches County, it was perhaps a hundred and fifty miles back east to Nacogdoches town, the county seat. In contrast Bryan and Isaac Young had to go only about seventy miles to the east and north to Fort Warren to make the deal legal. For this same reason the following February, John Neely and Margaret went to Forts Bonham or Warren in Fannin County to get married rather than make the longer journey to Nacogdoches.

There has also been considerable historical confusion about just who made the original Dallas town plat, or if Bryan actually created that confusion of cow paths. The Bryan-Young deal indicates the first plat was made earlier in 1842 by surveyor Lawrence W. Fern, rather than by James P. Dumas in 1844, as indicated in previous histories.

Dr. Britton thinks that Isaac Young may have been Bryan's original investor. The lot was at the corner "of Main and Broadway," which would now be the Dealey Plaza.

In one of her interviews when she was in her nineties, Mrs. Bryan told of the only time she was frightened by Indians. It happened on a day in early spring 1843. John Neely was using his Old Testament wooden plow (bois d'arc is very hard wood) pulled by the Indian pony to break ground for planting corn in a field about where President John Kennedy was killed one hundred and twenty years later. His bride was washing clothes. About two hundred Comanche horsemen came across the ford led by the war chief Pochanquarhip or Buffalo Hump.

Although her early years are not precisely documented, Margaret Bryan seemed to have spent most of her life, before she came to Texas in a big wagon train, in relatively civilized Calhoun County, Illinois. The Indians she had seen before had been under controlled conditions.

Bryan called from the cornfield to his wife that there was no cause for alarm. He dropped the reins of the plow pony and walked out to meet the visitors, shouting greetings in Comanche phrases and in sign. And Pochanquarhip, blood enemy of most Texians, slipped from his war-horse and embraced the founder of Dallas.

The Bryans' first crude home by the Trinity served as a store, the wares including a barrel of whiskey. It was also the post-office for any letters that might come that way. The Comanches showed up too early in the spring of 1843 to suit Bryan. He had hoped they would make a guest appearance the following August for President Houston's meeting with the wild tribes at Grapevine Springs, now the town of Grapevine, near Dallas. But the Comanches, even under Bryan's urgings, weren't good at keeping time schedules and didn't come back in August. Buffalo Hump's people traded tanned hides for coffee. The Comanches had acquired a taste for coffee. In the wild state they had no use for whiskey and called it "the fool medicine" of the "taibos" or whites. These horse Indians made attacks on wagon trains and other gatherings of palefaces on what they called the white folks' "big medicine day," that is on Sunday, because they had found that many taibos were befuddled in the early morning hours Sunday because of Saturday night's whiskey binges.

By early in 1842 Dallas was on Republic of Texas maps. There are several theories on the identity of the mysterious, unnamed as far as the first name, "friend" for whom Bryan titled his town. He had once been a lawyer and land developer in western Arkansas, although he said one of his real endeavors there was helping his Cherokee friends get legal claims on new land just across the line from Arkansas in Indian Territory (now Oklahoma). In Arkansas he had a friend, Joseph Dallas, who settled in what is now the Cedar Springs section of Dallas in 1843. There are a number of other "guesses" as to who was Bryan's "friend," none documented. George Mifflin Dallas, vice president of the United States, 1845–1849, is the one most often mentioned but it is unlikely that this Philadelphia lawyer was the frontiersman's friend in 1842.

Bryan's legal training probably enabled him to fight off the Peters Colony developers from taking the most valuable square mile in Dallas, the townsite by the ford on the Trinity.

Bryan did legal work when he and his father-in-law, John Beeman, went to Austin and persuaded the legislature of the brand-new state of Texas to create a Dallas County. This was in 1846. Once he was back in Dallas town, Bryan was the "commissioner" for organizing a county government. He sought no public office, elected or appointive.

In 1845 a second lawyer was in town. He was John C. McCoy, and he was some sort of legal representative of the Peters Colony trustees although he must have had a very agreeable personality for he never ruffled the feelings of the settlers.

McCoy was a native of Indiana. He had arrived in Galveston by water and said he had been told he could go up the Trinity to Dallas in a boat. When he found this was impossible he literally walked to Dallas. He said he came to the Republic of Texas because all his life he had wanted to live in a foreign country.

In 1845 Republic of Texas citizens voted on whether or not they wished to be annexed as a political district of the United States. In Dallas there were thirty-two voters. Only three voted against annexation, McCoy, Alex Harwood, and John Rawlins. McCoy claimed he even tried to organize a mob to protest the election, although in 1845 Dallas it couldn't have been much of a mob. Maybe just McCoy, Harwood, and Rawlins.

When it was certain that the Republic of Texas would cease to exist, McCoy said bitterly: "I had to walk the last three hundred miles or more to get to Dallas and now this annexation business is cheating me out of the right to live among foreigners. Texas would be better off as an independent nation. It is letting itself in for a lot of trouble becoming a part of the United States."

For weeks during the years 1849–1850 John C. McCoy was said to have been the only male resident of Dallas town. It must have provided a fertile subject for gossip for years thereafter. McCoy was about thirty and a bachelor. All the other men, including, naturally, John Neely Bryan ran off to either participate in the California Gold Rush or, in the case of several Dallas eccentrics, to dig for gold in the Wichita Mountains of Indian Territory near present-day Lawton, Oklahoma, not a promising area for gold mining.

John Henry Brown (1820–1885), a Dallas historian and early mayor, wrote: "The sole Dallas stay-at-home, John C. McCoy, was a lawyer who lingered to play a prominent role in Dallas." Brown didn't mean it that way but McCoy must have played a prominent role in 1849–1850 Dallas. Before all Dallas men except McCoy "went marching off to seek gold in 1849 Mr. McCoy was the butt of many jokes. Time proved him wise to stay at home."

Most of the Dallas men, including Bryan, came home from California broke. (Bryan made at least two trips to California.) Some of the gold seekers were intercepted by wild Indians or wilder white thugs and didn't return.

Getting back to McCoy, he and Bryan started the "library association" in Dallas, apparently with the books of the two most literate persons in town. McCoy was married in 1851 to a belle named Clara McDermott. For his bride he built the first frame home in Dallas. At the time other Dallasites lived behind walls of logs or even buffalo hides and mud.

McCoy was something of a socialite. In 1859 Dallas' first real hotel, the St. Nicholas, was opened with a dinner dance. Cockrell reported that "the grand march was led by Col. John C. McCoy (all prominent citizens were automatic colonels even if innocent of military service), the nestor of the bar, with a beautiful lady listless on his arm." (Why was McCoy's lady listless?)

McCoy was also clerk of the first court.

Cockrell said that Bryan had a larger home in 1850 (the Nacogdoches County census a few years before had him living on White Rock Creek) and it "was headquarters for everything that was happening. Bryan had become a man of influence, the central figure and prime mover in all things. A confidential agent of President Sam Houston on many occasions."

Cockrell said Bryan "spent some time in California, pretty

early in the Gold Rush for that country." Apparently he found
no gold and made most of the return trip home alone, as
Cockrell described it: "It would be difficult to conceive a more
perilous or lonely journey. Again we see that Bryan's knowledge of the Indians and their languages as the sesame to
friendship and comradeship."

He got home in time to supervise an election to determine a
permanent county seat. Dallas had been only the temporary
seat of government since '46. Dallas led with 191 votes, Cedar
Springs had 101 votes, and Hord's Ridge or Oak Cliff 178 in a
primary. In the runoff election Dallas won over Hord's Ridge,
244 votes to 216.

Bryan was magnificently equipped for starting a frontier
town. He didn't fit in well after his creation became structured.
As Mrs. Bryan said in one of her interviews: "I might get up
of a morning and shake out the bedclothes and he would be
gone." He was as restless as any wild Indian. It was during this
time that he may have accepted Jim Bridger's invitation to
come to Fort Laramie and serve as interpreter between the
Sioux and other Indian belligerents of the northern plains and
U.S. representatives. He seems to have had a radarlike sense of
direction in wildernesses and, of course, his knowledge of Indian dialects kept him out of a lot of trouble.

His long struggle with the land developers of the Peters
Colony to finally get a title in 1854 on his land must have
been very unsettling to his mind. He was probably tired of
serving as a free lawyer to ungrateful people. John Henry
Brown wrote that while Bryan was licensed as a lawyer in
Texas "he was too much engrossed with other cares to follow
his profession regularly. His legal training was, however, of
great benefit to others in drafting legal papers and as an ad-
visor to newcomers."

Bryan had sold whiskey for years but never overindulged in
it apparently until about 1854. As one old-timer described it,
"Neely began to tend bar on the wrong side." In other words
he became a drunk. Cockrell wrote on a difficulty that was to

send Bryan into exile from Dallas for about five years: "In Bryan's frenzied state of mind in 1855, he shot and wounded and thought he killed a man who, when intoxicated, had offered an affront to Mrs. Bryan . . ."

At this period in his life Bryan had a lot of time on his hands. He had sold or given away eighty-two town lots but there were still plenty of vacant lots left in his mile-square townsite. He sold these and his interest in a ferry boat franchise to Alex Cockrell for seven thousand dollars, a lot of money in those times.

Bryan took off for the Indian country, thinking he would be wanted for murder. Before he left he met another lawyer, perhaps McCoy, and "signed papers to take care of his business interests and his family during his absence."

Apparently enough was left over from the seven thousand dollars so that Margaret and the children didn't have to worry about money, even with Papa gone for five years. Maybe, they were glad to see him go for he had been making a drunken pest of himself. He got several letters during his absence from his wife and from Alex Cockrell. Could it be that they kept him in ignorance that there was no murder charge so he would stay away. The man he had wounded recovered completely, said that he was at fault and had no intention of prosecuting the founder.

In an old trunk Frank Cockrell found several of Bryan's fugitive letters to Alex Cockrell. The first of these was written under the heading of "Creek Nation, February 25, 1856":

"Mr. A. Cockrell: Sir, I received your letter of December 4 a few days since and I was very glad to get it. I have received only one from my wife. I am living with Jesse Chisholm in the Creek Nation, about forty miles north of Fort Arbuckle. Chisholm is a half-breed Cherokee and an old friend of mine. I have done nothing yet to make a living. I sometimes think it would be best for me to go into the western part of Texas and make a new home for I want to see my family and shall not be satisfied until I am again with them. I wish you to write to me and advise me in when it is safe for me to come home. I am surprised that Colonel Stone and others are turning against me. And I shall meet them yet when they least expect it and will then know the reason why they do so.

"Give my love to my wife and children and say I will be with them as soon as I can."

Cockrell was not only failing to write Bryan that it was safe to come home, he was telling the fugitive that he had other enemies such as Colonel Stone, whoever he was.

In 1858 Bryan was still writing despairing letters to Cockrell from Colorado and California mining camps. All ended with "give my love to my wife and children." And one from Stockton, California, said: "My respects to Mr. and Mrs. Cockrell and any others that you know to be my friends if I have any about. I remain your friend, John N. Bryan."

Cockrell's little history said that Bryan didn't return from exile to Dallas until 1861. Actually, he must have been back by August, 1860, when he signed papers in connection with the will of his father-in-law. He also returned to find that his friend Alex Cockrell had been killed by the town marshal in some silly quarrel. However, Mrs. Bryan had apparently inherited enough property and money from her father's estate that the family was comfortable financially.

There was no rest for Bryan though. His friend Sam Houston, Governor of Texas, had been forced from office because he had refused to take an oath of allegiance to the new Confederate States of America. There's no record how Bryan felt about Texas seceding from the Union. A man named N. H. Darnell had, according to Cockrell, been "on many of his scouts" with Bryan. Darnell in 1861 became the colonel of a Confederate cavalry regiment and fifty-one-year-old Bryan joined up as a scout.

There's no written evidence on what happened to him in the army, but Bryan was discharged after two years of service. Maybe he got drunk too often. He was in good enough shape to build a new house for the family on land "at Big Springs" on White Rock Creek.

Cockrell said that for about eight years Bryan gave no trouble to his family: "No longer did they fear he would leave home. He was frail and required attention." In 1872 he was on the speakers' stand when the first railroad train, up from Houston, arrived in Dallas. His mother-in-law had gone back to her old home in Illinois, and Bryan's daughter Lizzie married a man in Milton, Illinois. In 1872 Bryan, accompanied by two of his sons, made a railroad trip to visit Lizzie in Milton.

Then he started drinking heavily again. He was sent to live with John Neely Bryan, Jr., on a ranch near Llano for a while. His wife left him and went to live with one of their children.

Apparently, John Neely Bryan, Jr., had trouble putting up with his father on the Hill Country ranch and sent him home to Dallas. There one of the younger sons tried to take care of the founder but said that by 1877 the old man (sixty-seven) was getting violent and refused to sleep in a house. The family obviously wanted rid of him. John Henry Brown, the historian, was by then a state legislator and general big shot, and he wrote a letter to Governor Richard Hubbard asking that Bryan be made a patient in the State Lunatic Asylum, as the institution in Austin was called.

On February 1, 1877, a jury found the Dallas founder insane and "the county liable for the support of said lunatic. It is hereby ordered restraint and in the event it is ascertained there is a vacancy in the State Lunatic Asylum that he be sent to said asylum . . ." That's the last record on John Neely Bryan in the Dallas County archives.

On February 20, 1877, Bryan became a patient in the central building of the State Lunatic Asylum. This was three and a half stories of masonry construction in an architectural style sometimes called "Texas Italianate." At the time this was the largest building in Austin, even bigger than the old bat cave of a state capitol. The handsome 1857 asylum building is still one of the surviving landmarks of Austin and is used for offices and archives in a complex now called the State Department of Mental Retardation.

The superintendent at the time was a man of compassion and high intellect, David Robert Wallace, M.D., a native of North Carolina, who got his medical training at New York University and at the Pennsylvania Medical College. (See next chapter on Dr. Wallace.)

Perhaps Bryan was too far gone into alcoholism for therapy though. He died apparently in the central building of the asylum on September 18, 1877. At least that's the date I found on his asylum records. John Neely Bryan, Jr., later wrote the death happened on September 14. Where were Margaret and the children when all this was happening? If anyone in the family claimed the body there is no record of it.

Brown wrote this eulogy of Bryan: "He was not only the first settler of Dallas County. Soon after settling here he brought his library, respectable in extent, which was of great utility and was used by many. He visited Austin in 1846 and secured the creation of Dallas County—then organized it. He was a trusted medium through which President Houston communicated with wild Indian tribes. He was hospitable, large-hearted, freely spending his substance for others and for public uses, and at last, from impaired intellect and other causes, died destitute. The children of Dallas ought to erect a monument to his memory, for he was ever the children's friend and the friend of their mothers."

The asylum cemetery in Austin is between North Loop Blvd. and the 100 block of East 51st St. I thought Bryan might be buried there. There was no mention of Dallas' founder's death in any 1877 edition of Dallas newspapers I have studied or in the one Austin paper I saw in its September 1877 issues. How callous of Dallas, I thought, to let Dallas' founder be buried among ten acres of unmarked graves, especially since there should have been many Dallas inhabitants still alive in 1877 who had received gift downtown lots.

I thought there might be a map of the ten-acre graveyard.

The director of the state hospital refused to let me see the records at first and said that there was no map although, as I learned later, more than two thousand people had been buried in the ten acres. Some wood markers had been put up but grass fires had destroyed them.

Later I had to get an order from the county judge of Travis County before I could look at the records on Bryan in the asylum's archives. There wasn't much of a record. It was just written under the date of September 18, 1877, that this man "said to have been the first settler in Dallas County" had died "of intemperance." Nothing else. Not a word about what happened to his body. I would guess it might have been given to a medical school.

One of his sons was interviewed by the Dallas *News* in 1889 and said that the fact that Bryan sometimes gave away choice land in downtown Dallas cast him in the role of an eccentric to many: "My father owned everything in sight and he gave away many fortunes. In his last years he was an embittered alcoholic, deranged through recollection of lost opportunities and also as a result of hard, rough life on the frontier . . ."

17

"Friendship Through Eternity"

In the old Oakwood Cemetery in Waco there is a garden of sculpture which contains the life-sized statues of two tall, long-bearded men in frock coats. The stone statues face each other.

These are the sculptured likenesses on high pedestals of Richard Coke and David Robert Wallace, M.D. Coke dominated Texas politics during the years 1874–1885 as governor and then U.S. senator. Dr. Wallace has been called Texas' first psychiatrist. Coke and Wallace were good friends in life and they swore "friendship through eternity." They left money for the statues over their graves, one statue facing the rising sun and the other the setting sun.

During their long lifetimes they had many a friendly debate. And their facing stone likenesses in the graveyard give the impression that the debates are still going on.

One of Coke's first actions as governor of Texas in 1874 was to appoint his friend Dr. Wallace superintendent of the institution then called the State Lunatic Asylum. Wallace was one of the little-known characters in Texas history until the Timberlawn Foundation of Dallas, a nonprofit organization for education and research in psychiatry, financed publication of a life of the 1825–1911 medical doctor, written by the wife of a Dallas physician, Doris Dowdell Moore. She called Wallace "the first" and "eminent psychiatrist of Texas and the Southwest."

Wallace was from North Carolina. He earned his M.D. at the medical college of New York University. And he was such a brilliant student that he was offered the chair in New York's department of psychology. Instead he went to Texas to practice medicine.

Wallace was married to Susan Daniel in Independence, Texas, in 1857. They bought a home near that of Sam Houston, then between terms as a U.S. senator and as governor of Texas. A warm friendship developed between the old general and Texas' first psychiatrist.

Probably only a psychiatrist could appreciate the personality of the former President of the Republic of Texas and, before that, a "squaw man" living with Indians.

Houston's state papers and speeches, covering the years he was a Tennessee congressman, governor of Tennessee, and his Texas public offices, ran into thousands of pages, and the old general had a good, florid gift for prose. There are great speeches such as when he was forced out of the governor's office because he refused to swear allegiance to the Confederate States of America.

Houston asked Wallace to be his literary executor and to write his biography. Wallace wrote in a letter to Coke: "More than once Houston asked to have his private papers turned over to me. And more than once he asked me to write his biography."

Instead, after the general's death, someone in the Houston family, perhaps his pious wife, gave the Houston papers to a parson, Rev. W. C. Crane, who was also given authority to write a biography.

After reading the Crane version of the life of Sam Houston, Wallace commented: "Preacher Crane was no more capable of presenting Houston to the world as he really was than the parson can get a horizontal view of the Allegheny Mountains."

It's a shame that Wallace didn't write the Houston biography. He and Old Sam had spent hundreds of hours discussing things under the shady oaks of Independence. If Wallace had written the book there probably wouldn't be so many little mysteries about the life of the great Houston.

Mrs. Moore wrote of Wallace "in 1874 he found himself

superintendent of a rat-infested hellhole of human despair called the State Lunatic Asylum. It had been customary, from the time the asylum opened, for each successive governor to appoint his favorite doctor as the superintendent. Under such administrative upheaval little continuity had been possible and long-range objectives failed to materialize . . . David's first professional exposure to a lunatic hospital had been during his medical school days when he visited the New York City Asylum on Blackwell's Island. He remembered well the emotional impact . . . The rooms resembled cages with iron bars and most of the inmates wore camisoles or wristlets to prevent them from tearing off their clothes."

To cut down on the number of patients in the overcrowded asylum, Dr. Wallace sent harmless idiots, of which he found there were many, home to the care of their families. His concern was for patients he thought could be cured or helped.

There was no plumbing in the buildings in February 1874, and Wallace said: "I sent Mrs. Wallace to town for a lot of big black washpots and by building fires on the grounds we boiled enough water to delouse the patients and their clothing." He made every effort to serve the inmates "well-cooked and nutritious meals, and to keep the buildings, bedding and clothing of the patients clean and in good repair." In his report to Governor Coke, he said: "The largest liberty compatible with safety is to be allowed, and it is believed productive of the happiest results. It is thought better a patient occasionally escape than the asylum be converted into a prison.

"Insanity is a disease, its victims are sick people, and not the abodes of wicked spirits and malignant demons . . . No two cases are alike or amenable to the same means of control. Here it is that moral treatment finds occasion for the exercise of ingenuity."

Coke came to Texas in the late 1840s after he was graduated with honors from William and Mary College in Virginia. One of his uncles was a U.S. senator from Virginia. He came to Texas with letters of introduction from the then U.S. Senator Houston, and he practiced law in Waco. He served one term as governor of Texas and three as a U.S. senator. And the athletic, six-foot, three-inch Coke was known as "Old Brains" because of his intellect. His statue in Oakwood Cemetery has one hand fiddling with what looks to be a Phi Beta Kappa key.

He was married to Mary Horne in Waco in 1852. In the cemetery on either side of Coke's large stone feet are busts of his sons Richard, Jr., and Jack.

The boys died young, Jack from a fall while trying to break a wild horse and Richard, Jr., through some other misfortune. They look almost alike in the sculptured busts, hair parted mathematically in the middle and with neat mustaches.

18

Dallas' "Hot Dog Mayor," J. Waddy Tate

The only time I gazed on the elegance of J. Waddy Tate, "The Hot Dog Mayor of Dallas," he was at his desk in city hall in 1930 listening politely to the complaints of some formidable clubwomen. As he gave the clubwomen an audience he played with a yo-yo. It was a sure sign the mayor was bored when he played with his yo-yo.

His dress included a cutaway coat (also called a morning coat), a starchy white shirt with a large diamond stickpin in his black cravat, and a striped vest crossed by the heavy gold of a watch chain. Striped trousers and white spats, the spats affixed to shiny black shoes, and either a top hat or a derby completed his mayor's outfit, his working clothes.

He dressed a lot like the clotheshorse chief executive of New York City at the time, Jimmy Walker.

Tate was the last Dallas mayor under the commission form of government. With no city manager he was the big boss. He was a retired railroad executive, and he was able to give full time to city hall duties.

He earned his hot dog nickname because he served hot dogs and red soda pop at many parties for his followers in the Independent Voters Alliance.

While working for the railroad he became friends of two U.S. presidents, Theodore Roosevelt and William Howard Taft. Both invited him to the White House for parties several times. When J. Waddy ran for mayor of Dallas in 1929 he was opposed by the "establishment" but one of Texas' U.S. senators, Joseph W. Bailey, stumped for him.

He had a refrigerator in his city hall office and he served big glasses of cold buttermilk to visitors—whether they wanted them or not.

In his role as the working man's mayor he often quarreled with officials of a satellite community, Highland Park. He called Highland Park "a hideout for rich tax dodgers." Highland Park depended on Dallas for its sewer system. Once J. Waddy got mad and closed the sewers where Highland Park's emptied into the main Dallas sewers. He had the Highland Parkers begging for mercy.

With his own funds he bought a herd of perhaps fifty donkeys, all gentle beasts and broken to ride. And he left the burros in corrals in all the city parks. He said the burros were strictly for the amusement of the children of Dallas.

Dallas kids could go to the parks and ride burros for free. And sometimes J. Waddy gave hot dog parties for the youngsters.

The mayor looked a lot like W. C. Fields. Unlike the comedian he loved children.

With adults he could be a real curmudgeon. His cranky personality caused him to make some bitter political enemies.

When the gallant old curmudgeon left office in 1931 the new city administration did a terrible thing. The gentle burros in the parks were driven over to the zoo. And the burros were shot one by one and fed to the lions.

19

The Earl of Aylesford

"The Judge is Dead!" was a page-one headline in the January 14, 1885, edition of the *Pantagraphic,* a weekly newspaper published in the cow town of Big Spring, Texas. By "The Judge" the headline meant a thirty-six-year-old Britisher, Joseph Heneage Finch, seventh Earl of Aylesford.

He had come to live on a ranch about twelve miles northeast of Big Spring two years before and not long after the first railroad was built into the town. He came in a private car and under escort of the builder of the railroad, Jay Gould.

Aylesford brought along a half-dozen British retainers including his valet, William Benham. And in the baggage car were thirty blooded English horses, dozens of hunting dogs, and, as the *Pantagraphic* reported, "rifles, shotguns and other hunting paraphernalia in bewildering numbers."

Months before he had been in Big Spring to buy a cattle ranch. When he came back for good in 1883 the leading hotel in Big Spring didn't have enough rooms for him and his servants. Or so the management said at first. The earl made room by buying the Cosmopolitan Hotel.

He didn't like to drink alone. So he bought Big Spring's most popular saloon. He introduced himself to Big Spring society in 1883 by throwing a party to which everyone in town was invited.

He served as one of the bartenders. The party lasted for almost a week. He had paid six thousand dollars for the saloon. When the party was over he gave the saloon back to its former owner.

At the end of one of these marathon parties one of the town's leading citizens, John Birdwell, said to the Britisher:

"Your honor, we can't go around calling you all of your names. You got too many names. Way more than you need. So to save time and show our respect, we'll just call you Judge."

An issue of a Big Spring newspaper in 1885 said that "The Judge was revered by all. He died after an illness of two weeks."

The newspaper didn't mention that the earl's illness was alcoholism. A physician, Dr. Utter, said that Aylesford averaged drinking a half gallon of whiskey or gin daily during his years in and around Big Spring.

The correspondent of a Chicago newspaper who visited Aylesford's ranch in 1884 said there was a pile of liquor bottles as tall as the ranch house. It is symbolic that there is only one personal possession of Aylesford's in the excellent Heritage Museum in 1983 Big Spring: a corkscrew.

What was bugging this friendly, wealthy Englishman that he should devote so much of his time in Texas to heavy drinking?

The answer seems to be a sex scandal involving Lady Aylesford that drove him into West Texas exile.

In England of the 1870s the seventh earl was known as "Sporting Joe." He was a renowned athlete and reckoned one of the best polo players in Christendom. A historian of the Victorian court called him "a good-looking bounder."

Aylesford was a close friend and frequent companion of the Prince of Wales, the future King Edward VII. The Countess of Aylesford was also a "close friend" of the prince. He had been attracted to her, may have had liaisons with her, wrote her love letters. She saved the love letters, naturally.

The countess had a more serious love affair with a younger man, Lord Blandford, a brother of Lord Randolph Churchill and, of course, uncle to Winston Churchill.

In 1876 Aylesford went on a tiger hunt in India with the Prince of Wales. (They had a retinue of ten thousand soldiers, two thousand coolies, and twelve hundred riding elephants.) Poor Aylesford knew nothing of his wife's carryings-on with other men.

In the midst of his sport in India the earl received a letter from his wife, back in England, saying she intended to divorce him and marry Blandford, the future Duke of Marlborough. She said her boyfriend was going to divorce Lady Blandford.

Aylesford evidently loved his wife and hoped to persuade her to give up Blandford. He set out on elephant-back for the nearest railhead, on the long journey home.

"Joe has gone home heartbroken," said a friend also on the tiger hunt.

When the prince returned to England he put pressure to break up the romance between the countess and Blandford. He called Blandford "the greatest blackguard alive." Randolph Churchill championed his brother's cause, somehow got hold of the love letters the prince had written the countess, and threatened to publish them. The prince challenged Lord Randolph to a duel, which was never fought, but the two men became enemies.

Aylesford was talked out of a duel with Blandford. By this time he knew how false his wife had been. She was expecting Blandford's child.

Aylesford then decided to go to West Texas to hunt and drink.

It was no coincidence that he died on a January 13. He and his cowboy cronies in Big Spring started celebrating the new year. And the party lasted for almost two weeks.

On that January 13, Aylesford sobered up enough in his suite at the Cosmopolitan Hotel for a game of euchre. He was a brilliant cardplayer even with a lot of liquor aboard.

He didn't finish the game. He threw down his cards. And said: "So long, boys!"

And he died.

The Big Spring folks demonstrated gratitude by naming a street for The Judge. Only it is misspelled "Aylford" on all the street signs.

THE
MONEY SPENDERS

20

The Witch of Wall Street's Son

In Terrell, Texas, I stopped at the Rebecca Jarvis residence at 505 Pacific. There was no one at home. I wanted to inquire about E. H. R. Green's trousers and cork leg that the one-legged multimillionaire stored in a room of the mansion many years ago.

Although he never spent a night in the Jarvis manse, E. H. R. Green tried to establish it as his "home" for tax purposes long after he left Texas in 1911.

Mr. Green was the son of Hettie Green, called the Witch of Wall Street. Mamma Green was also described as the richest and most despised woman in America.

E. H. R. Green arrived in Terrell on January 27, 1893. His mamma had bought a rundown Texas railroad for him, the Texas-Midland. He deposited Ma Green's check for five hundred thousand dollars in a Terrell bank. As soon as they found the check was okay, he was elected a vice-president of the bank.

He was also dubbed "Colonel" Green by a Texas governor some time later. In those days any person who had five hundred thousand dollars in his checking account was an automatic colonel. (At one time, E. H. R. Green's wacky sister, Sylvia, had thirty-one million dollars in her checking account.)

He is remembered mostly as a playboy and the first to own an automobile in North Texas and as a financier of Republican politicians. And yet Green turned Texas-Midland into an efficient and profitable railroad.

In the city park in Terrell I took a look at an old private

railroad car said to have belonged to Texas-Midland in Green's time. The car was locked and later I told Audrey Patton that there was one or more blackbirds trapped inside. (Audrey is the decorative woman who directs the Carnegie Public Library in Terrell.)

The ancient wooden private car is being restored. It bears the number of 993. Green's private car was numbered 999.

In the mid-1890s Green had George Pullman design and build for him the luxurious private car which the colonel then labeled on both sides "Mabel." This was in honor of his future wife, Mabel Harlow.

Mabel was a beautiful redhead. Green lived with her for a time in his apartment over the former Harris Opera House, a building still in use on Terrell's Moore Street.

The Witch of Wall Street was shocked by her son's behavior. She spoke of Mabel Harlow as "Miss Harlot." Perhaps she was more shocked by the money "Eddie" spent on that private railroad car. Green later married Mabel. She was scorned in Terrell. She was snubbed in Dallas. Later in Florida Mrs. Green became one of the queens of high society.

Colonel Green's happiest years were spent in Texas. The tax laws of this state were then quite favorable to a multimillionaire. He was trying to avoid the tax laws of Florida and Massachusetts, where he had residences while keeping up the fiction that his official home was the rented room at the Jarvis mansion. He also voted in Terrell.

Green explored for petroleum drilling sites in Texas, but without much success. He used a pet burro for his "geologist."

He would turn the donkey loose in a field where he thought of drilling an oil well. And drilling would be where the donkey left droppings.

About 1909 Green built a three-story masonry home in Dallas at 2013 Commerce. After he left, the building eventually was owned by the city of Dallas and housed the health department. It was demolished in 1964 to make room for a city hall addition.

A 1910 writer visited Green's Dallas mansion and wrote: "The Hon. E. H. R. Green's bachelor quarters rival the Sultan of Siam's palace for luxury and elegance."

Edward Howland Robinson Green, the playboy's full name, was involved in the naming of a town called Cash, Texas. Up until recent years, Cash was a modest, one-general-store type of village. Now it's getting to be quite a little town, complete with a Mexican food restaurant in a new brick building and many new homes.

Cash was one of the towns founded in the 1890s when Colonel Green extended his Texas-Midland Railroad up from Terrell town into Hunt County. (Green started a nearby village on the railroad line and called it Hetty, for his mother, Hetty Green. Hetty is now a ghost town. Cash has endured.)

Green wanted to name what is now Cash in honor of a friend and business associate, J. Ansel Money. It would have been Money, Texas. Only Mr. Money declined for reasons of modesty.

"Well, by cracky, Cash is just as good as Money," said Green. "We'll name our town Cash."

An old-timer who lives between Cash and Hetty told me that Green drove the first automobile ever seen in Hunt County. This was, he said, in October of 1899.

So I took a look at some October 1899 issues of the Dallas *News*. And I found that Green was a passenger in the first motorcar to appear on Dallas streets.

His motorcar was a product of the St. Louis Gas Car Co. It was delivered in Terrell. It made its inaugural run on October 5, 1899, from Terrell to Dallas, a distance of about thirty-five miles. At the wheel was a factory representative, described by the Dallas *News* report as "a gentleman from St. Louis who is expert at handling these vehicles."

He must not have been too expert. For on Ross Avenue in Dallas the car ran over and knocked down a telephone pole "to the consternation of the Dallas telephone company."

The Dallas *News* report of October 6 was printed under big headlines: MR. E. H. R. GREEN'S CARRIAGE and DALLASITES WERE STARTLED! The story began:

"Hon. E. H. R. Green, the state Republican committee executive chairman, created a sensation in the city last evening. At 7:30 P.M. he rode up and down Main Street in a horseless carriage at the rate of 15 miles per hour."

The account said that Colonel Green and his driver left Terrell, where Green then "had elegant bachelor's quarters in the opera house, at 2:30 P.M."

Near the village of Forney the horseless carriage "was crowded off the road into a gulley by a farm wagon." And an hour's stop was necessary while a Forney blacksmith made some repairs.

During the five-hour saga from Terrell to Dallas "at least a dozen horses executed fancy waltz steps on their hind legs as the horseless carriage sped by."

The Dallas *News* report said "the vehicle is built like a phaeton. It is propelled by a gasoline engine of five-horse power. It consumed two quarts of gasoline on the 35 miles from Terrell to Dallas. The horseless carriage mowed down the telephone pole on Ross Avenue without injury to the machine or to its occupants . . ."

A further thought on reading the last two sentences in the 1899 Dallas *News* was that Colonel Green's first automobile should be copied into a 1983 motorcar if it could roll for thirty-five miles on two quarts of gasoline and knock down a telephone pole without damaging the car or its occupants.

A Dallas *News* story in the October 10, 1910, issue said that "Old Hurricane," as Green called his car, was running well, although no longer in the playboy's possession, and was being used mainly to pace two racing cars at the Dallas racetrack.

21

Silver Dollar Jim

The West ranch and oil field in the Kickapoo community of Madison County no longer reflects the unique personality of the late Silver Dollar Jim West.

If Mr. West had been there when I visited the ranch things would have been different. But he's gone. And no one gave me any gifts such as silver dollars or filled my car's fuel tank with casinghead gasoline or gave me a pound of sweet country butter. And now that Silver Dollar Jim is gone giant firecrackers are no longer heard exploding all over the ranch at night. He loved to pop firecrackers.

Mr. West, a multimillionaire, earned his nickname honestly. He would fill all his pockets with silver dollars and go around giving them away. This was only one of his eccentricities. He didn't give away all his dollars, though. In only one lode, his River Oaks mansion in Houston, 290,000 silver dollars were found stored after his death.

A friend, Peavine Jefferies, from the nearby Willow Hole community in Madison County guided me to the West ranch.

First we talked with A. D. Brown, who operates the West oil field and lives in a frame house which was Silver Dollar Jim's "clubhouse." The decor includes a big safe set in concrete where Mr. West kept his silver dollars.

Peavine Jefferies once lived on a farm adjoining the West ranch.

"I had to sell out and move to another family farm in the Willow Hole community because I couldn't get any sleep when Mr. West was at his ranch," said Peavine.

It seems that Silver Dollar Jim was much given to daytime slumbers. He spent his nights getting into mischief and making a lot of noise.

There is a high tower near the clubhouse. It served to hold loudspeakers from which country and western music sounded loud enough to be heard for two miles and always blared at night when Mr. West was in residence.

"He also liked to shoot firecrackers at night. And I mean big and loud firecrackers," said Peavine Jefferies.

Mr. West had a trailer which was a rolling sound system for his country and western records with those by Hank Thompson and Willie Nelson favored.

Peavine said Silver Dollar Jim would hook up the trailer after setting the records to play as loudly as possible. And then he would drive through nearby towns such as Madisonville and North Zulch from about midnight to maybe 4 A.M. and serenade the townspeople. He also had a record which sounded like a steam locomotive, cracking on all steam at about ninety m.p.h. and with the clackety-clack sounds of steel wheels on steel rails. He would play "train sounds" in towns which had never had a railroad. And you can imagine how these people felt waking up, say around 2 A.M., and hearing a train apparently roaring along in the night, complete with whistles.

Mr. West seldom got in trouble in those towns at night for causing disturbances. For he'd usually given fistfuls of silver dollars to night watchmen and police on late duty. One of his pranks was to stop in a town and find a parked police patrol car that wasn't being watched. He would then tie long strings of big firecrackers on the back bumper, the firecrackers to be ignited by a delayed fuse. Then he would loaf around hoping that some policeman would jump in the patrol car and take off about the time the firecrackers began to explode.

On a ridge near Jim's old clubhouse is the ranch house which he had constructed of steel and solid mortar, no doubt to guard another storehouse of silver dollars. Also on the ridge is Jim West's former dairy.

In Mr. West's lifetime a farmer operated the dairy on the shares. The ranch furnished the milk cows and the farmer could keep all the produce of the dairy except the sweet country butter.

Silver Dollar Jim was partial to butter. He took his own butter to cafes. On his excursions with his sound system trailer he would take along several hundred pounds of butter on ice and give butter to friends and when he ran out of friends to strangers.

"If it weren't that I didn't like to sleep to the rhythms of country and western music I would have liked neighboring with Mr. West. For he kept me in butter and casinghead gasoline," said Peavine. "And almost every time he saw me he gave me a silver dollar."

22

The Wild Flowers Man of the Oil Fields

Perhaps Texas wild flowers were Edgar B. Davis' Mojo Hand. Anyway, he was a different man after he fell in love with Texas wild flowers. And he used them to find oil fields in the most unlikely places.

He seems to have been a busy moneygrubber in his early years. He made a million dollars in shoes before he was thirty-five in his native Brockton, Mass.

He went off to Burma and made another million in rubber.

In Texas he not only made millions, he also developed a new talent for giving away many millions.

For example, there was the picnic on a warm evening in July 1926. At the picnic Edgar B. Davis gave about $7 million to his friends.

The scene was an outskirt of Luling, Caldwell County, Texas, under high trees on a shore of the spring-fed San Marcos River. There were more than twenty thousand guests.

Toward the end of the party Edgar Davis made some dead-pan announcements from a bandstand.

He said he was giving $5 million to the three hundred employees of his United North and South Oil Company.

He also said he was giving about $2 million for public installations, much of it for a 1,223-acre complex where Caldwell County farmers would be taught scientific agricultural methods, and where they would be provided with the foundations for beef and dairy herds and with plantings for orchards and hardwood and pine forests. These farmers had been mostly dependent on one crop, cotton. He gave money, too, for a "town forest" in Luling, the forest to include a clump of farkles. He had noticed in Switzerland that each town had its own municipal forest. He thought it a good idea.

Included in the $2 million grant were funds for two golf and tennis clubs, two swimming pools, and two gymnasiums.

For the picnic, Davis bought 140 acres along the San Marcos River. Two name bands were there for dancing. And there were a number of opera singers to entertain, such as the Metropolitan Opera tenor Richard Crooks.

The menu included forty thousand pounds of barbecued beef and fried chicken and such after-dinner offerings as seven thousand cigars.

The picnic was Davis' way of celebrating the sale, for $12,750,000, of his discovery oil field in Caldwell County. He said that the millions he realized from selling his oil field to a major petroleum company had not come "through any virtue or ability of mine, but has been given in trust. And I am now determined to discharge some measure of the trust that has been reposed in me."

He said he was trying to live according to the teachings of Jesus Christ. He quoted Christ's admonition: "For what is a man profited, if he shall gain the whole world, and lose his own soul? Lay not up for yourselves treasures upon earth, where moth and rust doth corrupt, and where thieves break through and steal. But lay up for yourselves treasures in heaven."

At times Edgar Davis weighed as much as 250 pounds. He was six feet, four inches in height, and he was quite agile. In Massachusetts he had been a high school football star. He wanted to go to Harvard and play football. However, when he was a teenager he had been required to go to work in the Davis family shoe factory.

This shy, muscular, mostly bald, blue-eyed behemoth of a bachelor listed his profession after he came to Texas as a "Faith Wildcatter." He spent his last thirty-three years in Texas. And he came to consider himself a Texan. When Massachusetts sued to collect state income tax from him he said: "I would no more lie about being a Texan than I would lie about anything else." (The state of Massachusetts sued him for $700,000 in state income taxes and he finally had to pay $200,000.)

Davis realized more than $35 million from his Texas petroleum explorations through the years. This is an amazing sum considering that in those times gasoline sometimes retailed in Texas for as little as eight or nine cents per gallon.

He gave $89,000 over a long period for annual awards for the best paintings of Texas wild flowers and for the best essays on wild flowers.

He believed that God, through the agency of wild flowers, guided him to his numerous petroleum discoveries. For he usually drilled where geologists thought there was no oil.

Davis declared that the beauty of the blossoms of Caldwell County, where the climate is kind and some wild flowers are in bloom the year round, gave him courage to carry on his drilling operations when he was heavily in debt.

He said the wild flowers of Caldwell County "sustained" him when he drilled six dry holes before finally hitting the wildcat well, the start of the original oil field which he sold for $12,750,000.

He believed that God had commissioned him to rescue Caldwell County farmers from dependence on the whimsicalities of cotton farming. And his Edgar B. Davis Agricultural Research Center was designed to combat the evils of the one-crop system. The 1,223 acres had seventeen units. One was a herd of registered dairy cattle and a milking parlor to produce certified milk, certified milk then being a novelty in Texas. There was a poultry farm with five thousand English white leghorns, each hen soon averaging two hundred eggs a year. There was a herd of registered beef cattle, and a flock of high-grade sheep. There were several hundred pecan trees on the property and more were planted. Soon fifty thousand pounds of pecans were being produced annually.

Young people were paid to work and learn at the Agricultural Research Center.

The seventh well he drilled in his first oil field was called Rafael Rios No. 1, this being a reference to an old Spanish land grant. By that time the six dry holes had used all of the million he had made in Burma as the operator of one of the first American-owned rubber plantations there.

While Rafael Rios No. 1 was being drilled, Davis became indebted to almost everyone who had any money in Caldwell County, most of all to the Luling banker, Millard Ainsworth.

The creditors tried to keep faith with this strange giant who had pumped $1,500,000 into the local economy.

Still, expenses for the seventh wildcat well finally caused him to run out of people from whom he could borrow. Then he remembered he had $80,000 in British government bonds, left over from savings made as a young man in the shoe manufacturing business in New England. He had an uncanny ability to make money in any business endeavor he tried. And yet he was careless with money. He found the $80,000 in British bonds stuffed in an old suitcase.

With the $80,000 he paid off most of his debts and continued to drill the seventh wildcat.

He had selected the site for Rafael Rios No. 1 in his usual way. He walked out in a field of Indian blanket and other wild flowers, studied the plants for a while, and then he yanked up one blossom, smelled its fragrance and said: "Drill here!"

Weeks later he was sitting with two friends in an open touring car near the seventh wildcat. He had used up all resources again. It looked as if he had another dry hole.

A column of oil shot up from Rafael Rios No. 1. The torque of the petroleum column broke the crown block of the derrick. In the open automobile Edgar Davis and his friends received a petroleum shower.

The friends reacted predictably. They got out of the car and shouted and jumped around.

Davis was calm. He walked out into the field until he came

to flowers that hadn't been sprayed by oil. He kneeled in a flower bed and seemed to pray.

He continued to select drilling sites with the aid of his friends, the wild flowers. The discovery well settled down to one hundred fifty barrels a day. It was followed by some real gushers. In two years among the prairie flowers he developed an oil field twelve miles long and two miles wide.

It was producing fifty-seven thousand barrels a day when he sold it.

He then put together a smaller field in another part of Caldwell County. He sold it for $4 million.

There was no picnic after this sale.

He decided he had been wrong in the public display at that multimillion-dollar picnic. And he quoted these words of Jesus Christ: "Take heed that ye do not your alms before men, to be seen of them: otherwise ye have no reward of your Father which is in Heaven. Therefore when thou doest thine alms, do not sound a trumpet before thee, as the hypocrites do in the synagogues and in the streets, that they may have glory of men."

No trumpets sounded. Yet Davis gave more than a million dollars in bonuses to his employees from proceeds of the sale of the second oil field.

He believed in reincarnation. He paid a large sum to a dramatist named J. Frank Davis to write a play called *The Ladder* on the theme of reincarnation. J. Frank Davis was no relation to Edgar Davis but they had been classmates in high school in Massachusetts. Frank Davis had been a worldwide reporter for newspapers, a writer of fiction for national magazines, and one of his plays, a melodrama, had been given four hundred performances on Broadway.

When he wrote *The Ladder,* though, his health was poor. And it was a difficult assignment trying to voice Edgar Davis' philosophy for the stage.

Mrs. Hazel Muenster of Luling, Edgar Davis' longtime secretary, read *The Ladder* several times. She said in 1975: "I had a copy of the play but lost it. Even if a fresh reading were possible it would still be difficult for me to describe *The Ladder* meaningfully. For it was a confused and mixed-up thing. It was a bad playscript, I think."

Mrs. Muenster said she told the boss she didn't like *The Ladder*. Still, the Faith Wildcatter believed in the "message" of the play. He went to New York City and financed a production on Broadway with Brock Pemberton as producer and director. Pemberton was given a generous budget for the cast and for operation.

The New York drama critics confirmed the judgment of Hazel Muenster of Luling. They called it the worst play ever seen on Broadway.

Edgar Davis kept *The Ladder* in that Broadway theater for more than two years. His Texas banker, Millard Ainsworth, guessed that about $2 million was lost on the play.

For the last year or so tickets were free. And most of the "customers" came to the theater to get in out of the weather or to sleep. The theater became a haven for bums.

Davis didn't seem discouraged. He said that 300,000 people saw *The Ladder* and for that his millions were well spent.

After the "long run" on Broadway, Davis closed the play. Even with offers of financing he couldn't persuade Hollywood to film his "message." He went to England to try and interest J. Arthur Rank in doing a movie version of *The Ladder*. The British film baron said no.

Under the guidance of the wild flowers Davis made more oil strikes. But he continued to give away much of his revenue.

Then the wild flowers began to fail him. He had apparently lost his Mojo Hand. He had a costly series of dry holes.

He was in his seventies and almost broke. His health began to fail.

There was plenty of hospitality in Luling and Caldwell County.

Banker Ainsworth and other friends offered to raise a stake of at least a half million dollars to finance Davis in petroleum exploration, or whatever he wished to do with the money. He said no.

The only home he'd had in Luling, called "Under the Oaks," had burned. He moved into a small house on the Edgar B. Davis Agricultural Research Center. The center was the most enduring thing he created. By 1983, it had expanded and was serving the farmers of two other counties in addition to Caldwell County.

At the center, Davis had a bad fall. Then a severe illness. He moved to a modest dwelling in Luling to be near his medical doctors.

He died in Luling on October 19, 1951, at age seventy-eight.

He never joined a church, although he gave money to almost every church in Caldwell County. He had asked that there be no eulogizing. Still, every preacher in Caldwell County spoke at his funeral.

He had been a composer of hymns. Hazel Muenster and Mrs. W. C. Bouldin sang one of his compositions at the services.

Although the house was gone, the yard of "Under the Oaks" was like a park. He was buried there. The inscription on his gravestone was simple. Other than the dates of his birth and death it read: "Edgar B. Davis, a Man of Faith."

In his last years he wrote essays for national literary magazines. One, published in the *North American Review*, had this to say:

"The fundamental trouble with the world today is the spirit of hate and envy which finds expression in selfish seeking after the first place; in greed, in wars for fancied economic and political advantage, in lack of consideration for the other fellow —and generally in placing a higher value upon a material thing than upon those of the spirit."

23

Girl from a Half-Million-Acre Ranch

Electra (population about four thousand), an oil and cattle town in Wichita County, Texas, was named for a glamorous girl, Electra Waggoner, later Mrs. Electra Waggoner Wharton Bailey Gilmore.

Her father, W. T. Waggoner, owned the half-million-acre ranch which encompassed the town site of Electra, called Waggoner originally. Then, in 1902, the inhabitants of Waggoner got up a petition to have the town's and post-office's name changed to Electra, for the beautiful cowgirl.

Electra was well educated and willful. While on a world tour with her parents, she displeased them by having a butterfly tattooed on one of her shapely legs. This happened in China.

She was given a ranch of several hundred thousand acres for a birthday present. She called her personal ranch Zacaweista, actually a botanical name for a kind of grass. Electra, incidentally, was named for one of her grandfathers, a famous old cattleman Electious Halsell.

By 1919, W. T. Waggoner's cattle kingdom was planted in producing petroleum wells—in fact, the half-million acres in six Texas counties are still pumping a lot of oil in 1983.

The Waggoners had a home in Fort Worth, and Electra personally acquired one of the real Turtle Creek mansions in Dallas.

She was one of the first girls in Dallas to have a complete trousseau from Paris before she was married, first to a Philadelphia socialite, A. B. Wharton.

She was Neiman-Marcus' first customer to buy twenty thousand dollars' worth of clothes in a single day. And Mrs. Carrie Neiman told me that Electra came back the next day and got about twenty thousand dollars' worth of other things she'd forgotten.

If you want to see where Electra lived in Dallas, drive by and take a look at 4700 Preston Road, an estate backing on Turtle Creek.

Life then at 4700 Preston Road was just one big, exciting house party.

Guests included socialites such as Ann Morgan, daughter of old J. P. Morgan, and politicians of the likes of Theodore Roosevelt, and New York matinee idols such as Lou Telegen and Carlyle Blackwell.

One of the most successful house parties started at 4700 Preston Road and wound up two hundred miles to the west at Zacaweista. On the ranch the timing was right for Electra's guests, mostly from the East, to watch an oil well gush with such savage force that it blew off the crown block of the derrick.

Carrie Neiman said that almost every day when Electra was in Dallas, Neiman's would send out large stocks of dresses for the girl's selection. The dresses would have to arrive in the original packages from Paris or New York, for she refused to consider a dress that anyone else had tried on. She rarely wore a dress more than once.

Her dressing room was like Neiman's stock room. One long closet was filled with fur coats. Her shoe cabinet usually held 350 pairs of shoes. And she had a new pair of shoes delivered to her daily, either from Neiman's or from a New York bootier.

Electra was born in 1882 in Decatur, Texas, the same year her father was building a castlelike house that still stands on a hill in the eastern reaches of the town.

She is not to be confused with her niece, a world-famous sculptor, Electra Waggoner Biggs. Mrs. Biggs now lives at

Zacaweista Ranch. The September 13, 1982 issue of *Forbes* magazine listed Mrs. Biggs as one of the wealthiest women in the United States, and on the same list was one of Electra No. 1's descendants, Albert Buckman (Buck) Wharton III, of Vernon, Texas. The first Electra died on Thanksgiving Day, 1925, in New York City. She was only 43. She had lived life to the fullest.

BITS AND PIECES

24

Miss Ima Hogg

A New York socialite while on a visit to Houston said: "Miss Ima is one of the few people to whom I genuflect."

She was speaking of Ima Hogg, one of the great ladies of the century.

Miss Ima died while on vacation in London on August 19, 1975. Before she left I spoke with her. I was wondering what a ninety-three-year-old lady would be doing in Europe. I didn't ask the question that crassly. Yet Miss Ima responded rather sharply:

"I'm going over there to see some plays and hear some good music, stupid."

She was born July 10, 1882, in Mineola, Texas. When she was nine years old her parents, Governor and Mrs. James Stephens Hogg, and her three brothers, moved into the governor's mansion in Austin. Jim Hogg became the first native-born governor of Texas and one of the best.

It was probably during Governor Hogg's campaign for election that the slander was started that he had twin daughters, Ima and Eura Hogg!

Miss Ima suffered much from her parents' choice of her Christian name. And the myth about Eura made it even harder to bear.

Actually she was named for the heroine in a long epic poem written by her uncle, Thomas Elisha Hogg.

Jim Hogg was one of the first investors in the Texas Company (Texaco), and he made other fortunes from his law practice and from the oil fields on the family ranch, near West Columbia in Brazoria County.

Miss Ima and her brothers gave much of their wealth for worthy causes. As an example, more than thirty-three years ago she established and financed an institution for child psychiatry, the Houston Child Guidance Center. She turned her grand, fifteen-acre estate, Bayou Bend, over to the Houston Museum of Fine Arts, complete with $750,000 to maintain the museum, its paintings, and an outstanding collection of unique 1800s Texas furniture. She restored parts of historic Texas villages and one whole hamlet, Winedale in Fayette County. Winedale is now an outdoor museum of an early German settlement and also a study center for the University of Texas. (The university has received millions of dollars in gifts from Miss Ima and her brothers.) She was one of the organizers and principal financial backers of the Houston Symphony Orchestra and she caused world-famous conductors from Leopold Stokowski to André Previn to become directors of the orchestra, not just guest conductors.

As I said before, she could speak sharply when aroused. Once, referring to an extremely wealthy Dallas man, she said to me: "Why doesn't that old son of a bitch do something for Dallas? He's tight enough to skin a flea for its hide and tallow."

She caused two of her parents' homes, their honeymoon cottage in Quitman, Texas, and the old ranch home in Brazoria County to be converted into public parks.

Before she died she had plans to restore some of the old buildings in the tiny village of Omen in Smith County. Mainly this was because her brother Will Hogg had gone to the Summer Hill Select School there. This was a prep school with such rigorous academic standards that its graduates were accepted without question by Ivy League universities. Professor A. W. Orr, who ran the school, told parents of his students: "No report sent from here means the student is doing well, for if a

student can't be aroused we send the sluggard home and tu-
ition will be refunded."

Will Hogg became an outstanding lawyer and like Miss Ima
was most philanthropic. Miss Ima said:

"My father always said that Professor Orr and his wonderful school had a lot of influence on my brother's character. It
is a shame more prep schools today don't have such impecca-
ble standards."

Miss Ima got a little angry with me when I wrote about the
old "ostrich race" hoax involving her father. The good-natured
hoax was a favorite amusement of Texas newspaper writers in
the 1890s.

When he was governor, Jim Hogg had two pet ostriches
called Jack and Jill. The governor, in his prime, weighed
around 250 pounds. W. D. Hornaday, the Dallas *News*'s chief
capitol correspondent in Austin, had an idea for a joking
story when an Australian came to town to exhibit some ostriches. Hornaday wrote a gag story that the Australian visitor
had challenged Governor Hogg to an ostrich race. And the
governor had accepted and would ride as a jockey on either
Jack or Jill. The story didn't mention that the governor
weighed 250 pounds. Now just about everyone in Texas knew
that the story was a spoof. But the yarn got on the wire services, and newspapers all over the United States and Europe
took it seriously.

From reading the Dallas *News* at the time you can't tell
whether or not the Sultan of Turkey and the King of Zululand
really wanted to enter birds in the Austin ostrich race. Yet
there were apparently serious stories about these challenges
and others from ostrich fanciers all over the world.

Hornaday finally ended the gag by writing that the race had
been called off because of injuries to Jack and Jill.

Miss Ima scolded me: "Why did you have to mention that
eighty-five-year-old joke? It wasn't very funny eighty-five years
ago."

It turned out, though, that she had fond memories of her father's ostriches, Jack and Jill:

"Father fenced off an area about the size of a city block near the governor's mansion for the ostriches to run in. They were fascinating creatures, especially just before a storm. Then they would do a strange, rhythmic dance. They were certainly an attraction except to horses. Horses were scared of them."

She said Jack and Jill caused carriage horses to run away when the ostriches were doing their ballet before a storm.

Miss Ima said one of the ostriches was badly bruised while being moved from Austin to one of the governor's farms and died of the injury. The ostrich's mate, although apparently in good health, died soon after that. "We thought Jill died of a broken heart."

She said her father "believed unusual pets added to the spice of life—especially for children."

Jim Hogg's pets included a black bear, a wild goose, and a parrot. And he didn't go in for cliché titles for the creatures. For example, Polly was the wild goose and the parrot was called Jane.

Jane the parrot was Jim Hogg's favorite pet. When the governor came home in the evening the bird greeted him with soprano shouts: "Papa! Papa!" And then perched on his shoulder.

Judging by her photographs, Miss Ima was a gorgeous Gibson Girl type in her early years. And she was a very handsome woman even on that day in August 1975, when she died of a heart attack soon after getting into a limousine in front of her hotel in London.

25

The Henderson County Hamburger

It took me years of sweatneck research before I finally determined, at least in mine and in some other Texas historians' estimation, that Fletcher Davis (1864–1941), also known as "Old Dave" of Athens, in Henderson County, Texas, invented the hamburger sandwich.

People who helped me most in my research were Clint Murchison, Jr., of Dallas and Kindree Miller, Sr., a fifth-generation potter in Athens. Fletcher Davis was Mr. Miller's uncle.

A reporter for the New York *Tribune* wrote from the 1904 St. Louis World's Fair of a new sandwich called a hamburger, "the innovation of a food vendor on the pike." By "pike" he meant the World's Fair midway.

Clint Murchison, Jr., had sent me a big picture of the 1904 World's Fair midway with "Old Dave's Hamburger Stand" marked apparently by Clint's grandfather, John Murchison, an Athens banker.

About ten years ago, Clint told me that his grandfather said that the as yet unnamed sandwich, the one now called hamburger, was served at an Athens lunch counter in the late 1880s.

Grandfather Murchison had vivid memories of the 1880s sandwich but recalled the name of the innovator only as "Old Dave."

Grandfather Murchison said the hamburger pioneer's little cafe was next to the J. J. Powers drugstore (later Stirman's drug) on the north side of the Henderson County courthouse square.

The sandwich was described as the classic greasy hamburger except that it was served with just-out-of-the-oven slices of home-baked bread rather than on a round bun.

Banker Murchison had traveled over much of the United States in the late 1880s and 1890s. He said he never saw another sandwich similar to Old Dave's. He said Athens folks were so intrigued that they raised a sum of money to send the sandwich virtuoso to the World's Fair.

Now "Hamburger University," the McDonald's food chain research organization, has apparently worked hard on the history of the chain's principal product. And Hamburger University's conclusion is that an anonymous food vendor at the 1904 St. Louis World's Fair was the first to introduce the sandwich to the public and was probably the innovator.

My problem was with the lack of memory about Old Dave's full name, in the case of Grandfather Murchison, and the sloppy reporting done by the 1904 New York *Tribune* writer who apparently just wanted to express his relish for the sandwich and to hell with the guy who made it.

I thought that there might be something about Old Dave being sent by the citizenry to the fair in 1904 editions of the Athens *Review,* which in 1904 was a weekly. Dick Dwelle, boss of the *Review,* turned over his 1904 files to me for about a week.

Old Dave's trip to St. Louis wasn't reported in 1904 in the *Review.* But then Kindree Miller heard of my quest through one of his friends, Albert Rierson. Athens had been famous for pottery since the 1860s, and the Miller pottery works has been in Athens for a century. I met Kindree Miller in his office at the pottery works. And he told me:

"Old Dave was Fletcher Davis, by trade a potter. He came here from Webster Groves, Missouri, near St. Louis. He wrote to my father for a job and he got off the train somewhere between Dallas and Tyler and he walked all the way, more than fifty miles, from the railhead to Athens. For some reason people here called him Old Dave at the start although he was still in his twenties when he got here in the 1880s. We called him Uncle Fletch after he was married to my mother's sister, Recinda (Aunt Ciddy) Allison.

"Uncle Fletch was a tall, athletic fellow. He was a turner in our pottery works but he would volunteer for jobs on the side. No one else wanted to tear down the old Henderson County jail. Uncle Fletch did it almost alone. When we got our first paved road in the country here, from Athens to Murchison, volunteers were asked to paint the middle stripe in that ten-mile road. Uncle Fletch was the only volunteer. He put cotton-picking pads on his knees and painted that center stripe. He played baseball on Athens town teams and then worked as an umpire when he got a lot of age on him.

"He was a natural and imaginative cook. He usually did the cooking at pottery picnics. The pottery business got slow in the late 1880s. And Uncle Fletch opened that little lunch counter next to the drugstore.

"I remember eating what was later called a hamburger at Uncle Fletch's cafe before I even started in the first grade.

"I never heard that story that the townspeople got up a pot to send him to the 1904 fair. It could have happened. But I think they just went up there on their own.

"When I was ten years old I went with my parents to the 1904 fair and to visit with our relatives. Uncle Fletch and Aunt Ciddy had rented a large house in Webster Groves, a St. Louis suburb. We stayed with them for maybe two weeks and we went to the fair almost every day and lived on hamburgers when we were there. Uncle Fletch had a good location, across the midway from a show featuring famous Indian warriors who had been talked into going on exhibit, including the old Apache, Geronimo."

Kindree said the sandwich was named during the fair. And both he and Grandpa Murchison said that Fletcher Davis was "interviewed by a fancy dan reporter for the New York *Tri-*

bune who also asked about the fried potatoes served with thick tomato sauce." Mr. Davis told the reporter that the sandwich was his idea but he learned to cook the potatoes that way from a friend who lived in Paris, Texas.

Clint Murchison, Jr., quoted his grandfather as saying: "Apparently the 1904 reporter thought Old Dave said Paris, France, in referring to the way the potatoes were cooked. For the New York *Tribune* story on the hamburger said the sandwich was served with french fried potatoes."

James A. Cockrell, a longtime editor of the St. Louis *Globe-Democrat,* thinks that scornful persons of German descent in St. Louis named Fletcher Davis' sandwich. Mr. Cockrell wrote me:

"I read the McDonald's hamburger researchers' story that the hamburger sandwich was innovated by an unknown food vendor at the 1904 fair. And it annoyed me that the New York *Tribune* reporter neglected to give the name of the innovator. What kind of a newspaperman was that guy?

"There are many people of German descent in St. Louis. I think these St. Louis Germans, or maybe only one of them, can be blamed for misnaming the magnificent Texas culinary creation—which deserves a more precise and flattering title.

"In St. Louis I've heard from persons, whose parents or grandparents came from the southern regions of Germany, say that northern Germans in the city of Hamburg were much given to eating ground meat, even in the distant past. Other Germans disapproved of the Hamburg ground meat freaks, especially the Hamburg types who liked raw ground meat. So the St. Louis Germans may have named the sandwich hamburger as a derisive gesture toward the barbaric, ground-meat gobblers in the city of Hamburg. It is certain that the people of Hamburg never got around to making a ground-meat sandwich. If they did it never caught on over there."

In 1974 the New York *Times* ran a story in which one Kenneth Lassen claimed that his grandfather Louis Lassen "invented" the hamburger sandwich in 1900 in a small cafe in

New Haven, Connecticut. And Kenneth Lassen complained that "the birthplace of the American hamburger, a tiny restaurant called Louis Lunch, was in danger of being replaced by a twelve-story medical complex . . ."

The New York *Times* story admitted that "a serious challenge to the title is a theory supported by the McDonald's Corporation, the nationwide hamburger chain. McDonald's historians have researched the problem and claim the inventor was an unknown food vendor at the St. Louis Fair in 1904."

After this New York *Times* story was published I got a letter from a New Haven native, Neil E. Shay, now of Dallas. He wrote:

"A pox on the New York *Times* for bulldozing honest facts out of the way. Let me state that Looie (Louis Lassen) sold one fine steak sandwich but it was never a hamburger.

"Up until I left the City of the Elms and New Ideas, New Haven, circa 1933, Louis Lassen was still serving this steak sandwich—never a hamburger. It was probably beef off the rump, cut in thin slices. And it was really something to take to bed with you around midnight after a social event."

When he heard about the New Haven Preservation Trust having plans to declare "the dimly lit, twelve-by-eighteen, Louis Lunch building a historic landmark," Clint Murchison, Jr., told me:

"Let's face it: if we let the Yankees get away with claiming the invention of the hamburger sandwich they'll be going after chili con carne next. The New Haven claim as the birthplace of the American hamburger is a phony one, and the quicker they tear down that old building and raise the medical complex the better."

Mr. Murchison is now planning a historic plaque at either Fletcher Davis' grave in the Athens cemetery or at 115 Tyler Street on the Henderson County courthouse square where the first ground beef was put between two slices of bread, garnished with, according to Grandpa Murchison, ground mustard mixed with mayonnaise, a big slice of Bermuda onion, and sliced cucumber pickles.

"When Uncle Fletch and Aunt Ciddy returned from staying the duration at the World's Fair there were several cafes making the new sandwich. So Uncle Fletch went back to firing pots in our pottery. He would cook hamburgers at picnics but he never reopened his little hamburger joint on the north side of the courthouse square," said Kindree Miller. "My uncle was proud of making the first hamburger sandwich but he never thought of commercializing on it."

26

In Uncertain, Texas

Uncertain, Texas, in Harrison County, on Caddo Lake, was so named because steamships in earlier days often had trouble mooring there. Originally it was called Uncertain Landing. Giant cypress trees grow in the watery approaches to the settlement. Paddle steamships had to wiggle through the trees to dock. It was also the site of an old fishing and hunting society, the Uncertain Club.

Now Uncertain seems a happy village with busy fishing camps, restaurants, a landing strip for small airplanes, and liquor stores.

Still, the longtime mayor, Fred Dahmer (he is in and out of office), told me: "There are many uncertainties here in Uncertain . . .

"Why, we're not even sure how many people live here. The state highway sign on the west side of town says the population is 202. That must include hound dogs and turtles and water turkeys and bobcats.

"Excuse me, for being uncertain again. This is a wonderful place to live. The human beings in our city limits are so hard to count because our corporate boundaries aren't certain. The lines zigzag through pine and cypress and farkle forests and allow for the sinuosities of Caddo Lake's shoreline and take in the sloughs and baygalls and, also, islands such as Taylor's Island here where my wife, Lucille, and I live."

Taylor's Island looks like a peninsula. Yet it is separated from shore by Taylor's Slough. And in times of high water the mayor really knows he lives on an island.

Fred Dahmer, who is in a wheelchair, has plenty of time now for being mayor and for playing a big pipe organ in his home. For years he was a mail carrier in this lake country. When the rains were heavy sometimes he had to deliver the mail in canoes, the occasions, for instance, when the bridges were washed out over Taylor's Slough to Taylor's Island, and to Whiskey Point.

One thing is for certain today in Uncertain. The incorporated village has no property taxes.

"We get funds for our city government by taxing utility companies," said the mayor. "And we run a very inexpensive government."

Curley's Marina Cafe in Uncertain belongs on my honor roll for backcountry catfish cafes. The little restaurant is very clean-looking and in 1983 had a yellow-haired waitress who was an adornment to any scene.

From the wide, porthole-shaped windows you look out on Caddo Lake with the big trees rising in singles or in moss-hung motts out of the dark mirrors of the water.

In Curley's kitchen there is often a triumvirate of cooks, Tizzie Mae Hicks, Mabel Rivers, and Rachel May.

Tizzie Mae, a member of Hudie Ledbetter's old church, the Lotta Church of God in Christ, is the real virtuoso. If she's not on duty the fare may suffer slightly, but the other cooks are her disciples.

In peanut oil, Mrs. Hicks fries the sweetest of catfish. She composes hush puppies free of heaviness, and her sweet-sour coleslaw is also memorable. First you have a plate of country fresh tomatoes and onions and celery and the beer comes cold from the kegs.

There are no churches in Uncertain. One theory is that no religious group wants to style its meeting place Uncertain. There are numerous churches outside the Uncertain corporate limits and off in the forests, such as the Old Border church, said to have spooks in residence.

27

An "Aspirin Taste" at Headache Springs

On the outskirts of Tyler, Texas, there is some city-owned land called Headache Springs National Park. As I keep telling Calvin Clyde, publisher of the Tyler daily newspapers, Headache Springs would be a prettier park if people didn't dump trash there among the tall pine trees.

There are a number of stories on how Headache Springs was named. Mrs. Loy J. Gilbert told me: "The waters of Headache Springs taste sort of like aspirin."

Maybe that's how the springs came to be so titled. Still the medicinal springs were called Headache at least as early as the 1861–1865 States War when there was a Confederate pharmaceutical laboratory there. And aspirin, or acetylsalicylic acid, wasn't introduced into medicine until 1893, or thereabouts.

Loy and Alice Gilbert guided me to the fountains of the springs which are about a quarter of a mile south of the park and a historical marker. And I pointed out to Mrs. Gilbert, president of the Smith County Historical Society at the time, that the historical marker has the erroneous information that the springs are north of the park.

The springs emerge from a big pipe in an arroya in which are planted one hundred-foot-high pine trees. The property is owned by Mr. and Mrs. Elmer Free. Mary Free, a daughter-in-law of the proprietors, brought a glass for us. We drank and there really is an acid taste somewhat like the flavor of Herman Dreser's 1893 innovation called aspirin.

"My in-laws claim that this water will cure just about any complaint," said Mary Free.

Perhaps the waters of the springs eased the pain caused by the bust-head whiskey made there in the old days.

A history of Smith County and Tyler tells that the Confederate medicinal laboratory was "in a large frame building on the Polinio Chireno Survey (a Spanish land grant) east of Tyler and on the Old Omen Road near what is called Headache Springs."

The laboratory was under the supervision of a Dr. Johnson from Virginia, his Christian name not included in any of the old accounts. Dr. Johnson made whiskey and "medicines from native plants: herbs, barks and roots."

These plants were near the springs from which esters of a salicylic acid could be derived. Maybe, old Dr. Johnson put together a formula for aspirin and didn't know it in his Headache Springs laboratory.

28

Ghosts of the Caddo Lake Country

In Jefferson, Texas, just up Big Cypress Bayou from Caddo Lake, there is an old (1850) hotel in New Orleans architectural style callel the Excelsior. The big rooms are graced with antique furniture and paintings, some of these originals from the 1850 version of the inn. Cissie McCampbell, the longtime resident night manager, was nationally famous for the delicious country-style breakfasts she cooked.

Some sensitive persons, including Ruby Britton, for years a maid and now one of the cooks, claim that the lovely hotel has ghosts in residence. The spooks are usually described as friendly.

One of the more frightened persons ever to spend a part of a night at the Excelsior was Steven Spielberg. He is the director of numerous motion pictures such as *E.T., Raiders of the Lost Ark,* and *Close Encounters of the Third Kind.*

Mr. Spielberg said he had an intimate encounter of some kind with one or more of the Excelsior ghosts.

Spielberg told columnist John Anders of the Dallas *News:* "There's an old hotel, the Excelsior, in Jefferson which really freaked me out. We pulled in there one night during the filming in Texas of *Sugarland Express.* And we dragged ourselves upstairs after a rough day. I swear my room was haunted.

"I made everybody wake up, pack up, and get back in the cars at about two o'clock in the morning. We had to drive twenty miles to the nearest Holiday Inn and everybody was hot at me.

"I should add that I am not normally superstitious."

Spielberg was upstairs in the east wing of the Excelsior. A number of guests who've spent nights in this, the oldest continuously operated hotel in Texas, have also complained of spooks. And Ruby Britton, when she was a maid, refused to go upstairs alone in the east wing because of what she described as a "headless man" in the room occupied for one night in 1878 by Jay Gould, the railroad builder and "robber baron." Gould signed the hotel register with a good likeness of a jaybird drawn at the end of his signature. He skipped without paying his hotel bill. He had been angry because the Jefferson citizens wouldn't pay a bonus in money and land for running his trains through town. He said unless he got the "bribe" he wouldn't put machine shops in Jefferson.

Former President U. S. Grant was a paying customer of the Excelsior on the night of February 7, 1883, and President Rutherford B. Hayes checked in on January 8, 1878, according to the hotel register which also contains the signature of Oscar Wilde.

A Shreveport woman wrote me in 1979 that "someone" kept pulling the covers off the high four-poster bed in which she was sleeping (she swore she was sleeping alone) in the Rutherford B. Hayes room.

A Fort Worth woman in the adjoining U. S. Grant room claimed that the bathroom contained an "unseen presence breathing heavily."

I've stayed in all the east wing rooms and have noticed nothing alarming. Oh, I did hear that "breathing" in the bathroom shared by both the Hayes and Grant rooms. Was this a ghost with emphysema? Nope, it's probably a sound from the old plumbing which includes a gargantuan bathtub set on legs shaped like lion's paws. And the sides of the tub are adorned with golden cherubs.

A Dallas man who has four university degrees and is a hypnotist claims he has a "sixth sense" for detecting the presence of disembodied human spirits. This fellow will be called "the Ghost Detective" from now on, for he makes his living as a dentist and he doesn't want his patients to know that hunting spooks is his "hobby."

He said he has seen "only twenty-five apparitions" in his lifetime but has heard and "smelled" other persons from the spirit world. Some time ago he said he spent a night in the north wing of the Excelsior and he complained: "A hard-breathing yet unseen-even-by-me presence worried me all night."

In the days of the Republic of Texas (1836–1846) Jefferson was the busiest river port in the new nation. It was built along the stream called the Big Cypress, the streets surveyed at right angles to that bayou. And the wharves were loaded with the products of the northeastern reaches of Texas, from there to be transported by side-wheel steamships to New Orleans or other Mississippi River cities by way of Big Cypress Bayou, Caddo Lake, and the Red River's flow into the Mississippi.

During the 1861–1865 States War Jefferson became a manufacturing center including a brewery. In 1867 it began using artificial gas for lighting, and ice was manufactured commercially.

It is a town of grand 1800s mansions, the materials and furnishings sometimes brought by the paddle boats from St. Louis and New Orleans.

In 1870, though, Jay Gould wrote on the hotel register: "The end of Jefferson! Grass will grow in your streets!" As recited previously in this narrative, Gould was mad at the Jefferson citizens when they wouldn't give him a bonus to establish machine shops for his railroad there. (He later got $100,000 from Dallas to bring his railroad to that little town.) Gould put the machine shops in Marshall about 20 miles on west from Jefferson. Main reason Jefferson declined after the 1870s, though, was that the U. S. Army blew up the "Red River Raft," which had been holding back the water upstream, and destroyed navigation in Big Cypress Bayou. After that, Shreveport, La., on the Red River became the big river port near the Texas border.

The Excelsior, with its New Orleans scheme of architecture, was built in 1850 by a Captain Perry (first name lost to recollection), a Mississippi River steamboat skipper and a friend and contemporary of Captain Henry Shreve, the founder of Shreveport.

One of the early owners of the Excelsior was Mrs. Kate Wood. Fred Fegans, a ninety-year-old black cattleman (he still handles the chores on his livestock farm), is the best and perhaps the only living authority on how the Excelsior was operated when Mrs. Wood and her daughter were the owners. And this was the period most of the distinguished guests showed up, including the two Presidents and John Jacob Astor and W. H. Vanderbilt and the 1880s British hippie and playwright, Oscar Wilde.

On his stock farm, Fred Fegans, a very intelligent person, told me: "My mother was a cook at the Excelsior in the days when the hotel was having some mighty important white folks as guests. And I sort of grew up there. When I was eleven years old I was given the full-time job of taking care of Old Frank, a huge white English bulldog who belonged to the Wood family, or I would say the Wood family belonged to Old Frank.

"Miss Lizzie Wood, the daughter, was a low, mighty heavy woman. And she really loved that fat, heavy slobbering old bulldog. When Old Frank broke off a tooth chewing on a bone his mistress had a dentist put in a gold tooth.

"Old Frank had a diamond-stubbed collar that I was afraid someone was going to take off him since that dog was good-natured. Only the diamond collar was pretty safe for I was around doing something for that dog most daylight hours. I would bathe and currycomb Old Frank three times a day.

"He slept up in Miss Lizzie's room and every morning I would take out his bedclothes and wash them and let them sun. And Miss Lizzie had me feeding that dog steak three times a day."

Fred Fegans said that when Old Frank died, Lizzie Wood

had a big funeral for him, and the pet was buried in Oakwood Cemetery near the graves of U.S. senators, governors of Texas, and a number of outlaws.

"Miss Lizzie had to get a square casket, and it was velvet lined," said Fred Fegans. "Old Frank's body was taken to Oakwood in a horse-drawn hearse with members of the family and friends following in other carriages. Miss Lizzie said she was sure going to miss Old Frank's gold-toothed smile. She said that. I never saw that bulldog smile."

The Excelsior serves only breakfast, but what a breakfast! The menu always includes memorable breads made from scratch, such as tiny biscuits and orange-pecan-butter muffins. And these are served with native East Texas jellies, such as mayhaw jelly. And thick slices of country ham are usually among the entrees.

Down on the Big Cypress Bayou shore, about a block south of the Excelsior, are the ruins of another 1850-model hotel, the Haywood House. This four-story inn was once billed as "the largest and most elegant hotel in Texas."

Now the Haywood is a wreck except that the brick walls may still be strong. There is a steep stairway, still mostly intact, leading to the second floor, where there are large suites with double parlors. On the stairway when I was last there was a "travellor," this being a form of an escalator with a stool attached to the railing on which guests could ride up and down.

The Ghost Detective said he visited the Haywood's ruins in 1962. And he found it was dominated by an evil presence. Some ghost smell, he said. And there was a nasty odor in the Haywood.

I told him that I thought the lobby of the Haywood House really stunk, but I blamed it on skunks with dens there in the winter.

It was in 1962 that Clarence Braden died. He was one of the wealthiest men in Jefferson. He was a onetime college professor, and included among the land and buildings he owned in Jefferson were the ruins of the Haywood House. Braden used the ruins as his "personal bank." He was careless with money. After his death it was found he'd left thousands and thousands of dollars in unlocked rooms around the town. Perhaps $30,000 in coins and bills were in the Haywood ruins. At one count it was found the old bachelor had stored in unguarded buildings 3,322 silver dollars, 31,213 half-dollars, and 63,890 quarters. Many of the coins were collectors' delights, and this count didn't include bills of sometimes lofty denominations.

He never tried to hide any of his money. He just left it lying around. He was a real absent-minded professor. Once he made a trip to Europe and brought back many packages of fine wines and expensive perfumes and jewelry, each one marked as a gift for a friend.

Only he forgot to deliver the gifts. After he died the packages were found stored in an office over a drugstore. Braden owned the building and used the upstairs office occasionally but never locked any doors. Churns, crocks, and cardboard boxes were his favorite places for keeping money.

The Ghost Detective said he went back in the Haywood House after Braden's money had been removed.

"Previously I'd actually ached when I went in that place because of the evil spirits and the nasty odors of the presence there. But when I came back right after the money had been found and taken away I sensed that the ghost or ghosts that had been there were no longer earthbound. All gone."

He mentioned that he'd just visited one of the most splendid nineteenth-century mansions in Jefferson "and the place was literally jumping with spirits, some of them not so benign. I could feel them especially on the many balconies of this historic house."

Scottsville, near Jefferson and Uncertain but off in a flowering pine forest of Harrison County, is a dreamy-looking village with a cemetery which is a park of beautiful sculpture, some of the art from Europe.

Once Carroll Shelby and I were driving in the Caddo Lake country and I offered him a five-dollar bet that the next person we stopped and talked with would admit he or she had seen a ghost recently. Shelby, the old race driver and sports car stylist, is a native of East Texas. He should have known better than take the bet, especially since I was at the wheel and could pick the person we spoke with.

Anyway, I decided our interview would be with an elderly fellow on horseback. He had some connection with the Old Border Baptist Church, just down the road from Scottsville. (I think this church was named when there was dispute over the location of the border between the Republic of Texas and the United States.)

The old horseman said: "I saw some boogers the other night down around the Old Border Church."

We also talked with a woman in Scottsville, a parishioner of the Old Border Church, who said flatly she often saw ghosts. She described these sightings in casual manner: "Not many folks can see boogers. You feel warm, steamy air. Onliest, I don't have to feel the warm steam. I see them boogers. I'm not afraid of them. You mention God's name and you don't see them no more. They go away.

"I've seen the ghosts of dogs. Not any dogs I ever knew. Just dog ghosts."

29

Up in Eunice's Room

Earlier in this narrative there was reference to the 1840s mansion called The Brick House which T. J. (Cap) Taylor bought for his bride in 1904.

Mr. and Mrs. Taylor's children, including the future First Lady, Mrs. Lyndon Johnson, were born there. And the children's mother died there.

The manse is in an L-shape with sixteen-inch thick masonry walls. And there are two wings. The staircase is outside but under the roofs of the back galleries. And the upstairs bedrooms have doors leading out on the second floor galleries. There is a lovely New Orleans-style courtyard with an old well, no longer functional.

Cap Taylor had a ritual connected with that well. He would go out in the courtyard very early each morning in a state of undress, pump a bucket of water, and pour the water over his head. When he was at home he never missed a morning doing this even during freezing weather.

The Brick House and surrounding livestock and pine tree farms are now owned by T. J. Taylor's widow and second wife, Ruth Taylor. And Ruth Taylor's nephew, Jerry Jones, and his beautiful young wife, Patricia, and their interesting children, Jett and Angela, also live there. Jerry Jones runs the farm.

In 1983 Angela was eighteen and Jett was thirteen. They believed they have shared their lives with a girl ghost.

When he was three years old, Jett, a handsome, yellow-haired, bold personality, started speaking of his unseen (unseen at least by all except Jett) playmate. She said she was an adult female. He called her "Oonie." Was his playmate Eunice Andrews?

Now for decades The Brick House had a resident girl ghost, or so had gone the story. As recited previously, the mansion was built for Major Milt Andrews who, among other endeavors, kept a general store at a Caddo Lake steamship landing called Port Caddo. The major had a daughter, Eunice, said to have been very good-looking.

One stormy night in the early 1850s Eunice Andrews was sitting by the fireplace in her room, the back upstairs bedroom. A bolt of lightning came down the chimney and killed her.

Since then there have been tales of strange goings-on in what has always been called "Eunice's room." It has been used only as a guest room. And guests usually don't want to sleep there a second time.

As mentioned previously, T. J. Taylor bought The Brick House from an elderly medical doctor, a collector of hickory nuts, among other eccentricities. T.J. and his bride must have heard the story of the girl ghost even before their purchase. And it is possible that the doctor used the bedroom for storing hickory nuts because folks were nervous about spending a night there.

Jerry and Patricia Jones say they never told "booger stories" about Eunice when Jett and Angela were growing up. And yet at age three Jett began talking about this spooky girl friend he called Oonie. Oonie certainly sounds like a diminutive for Eunice.

By the time he was ten Jett was calling his personal apparition "Miss Andrews." He said Oonie sounded too babyish.

Angela's earliest years apparently were undisturbed by manifestations of Eunice. However, since she was about twelve she has been the only person presently in the household who admits to uneasy encounters with Miss Andrews.

There is a huge bathroom adjoining Eunice's room but with

another door leading out on the upstairs gallery. Angela, pretty and intelligent, who has been winning Junior Miss charm and beauty contests since she was six years old, said that twice she has heard a "scary voice" calling her from "that room" when she was in the adjoining bathroom. And when she checked immediately there was no one in Eunice's room.

And once Angela said she came in the bathroom to brush her teeth only to find that her toothbrush was out of the rack and "flying" around in front of the medicine chest.

For an imaginative child Jett doesn't have much to say about Eunice's appearance except that she "is a sort of pretty girl in a long dress and her hair stands up all the time."

Jerry Jones said that Eunice "used to stay in her room." But now, according to Jett, "she's all over the place."

Once I drove up to The Brick House and all the cars were gone from the driveway. Jett was trying to launch a kite in the front yard. "Where is everyone?" I asked Jett, who was then four. "Oonie is here," replied the little boy.

Several adults claim they've experienced strange goings-on up in Eunice's room.

One of these is Tony Taylor of Santa Fe, N.M., T. J. Taylor's son. Mr. Taylor is certainly a sensible fellow but he has this to say about Eunice's room: "During storms I've heard some pretty weird sounds in that room, like girlish sobs. And this was on nights when there were no girls staying in The Brick House. Not live ones, anyway." Then he added jokingly: "I don't blame Eunice for haunting that room. She was treated unfairly by the elements. If you're sitting by a cozy fire behind thick brick walls you hardly expect to be hit by a bolt of lightning."

I also talked with Ruth Taylor's sister, Mrs. Pauline Allison, one of the Garden Club women who own and manage the Excelsior Hotel in nearby Jefferson. Mrs. Allison said she had spent several nights in Eunice's room. She remembered one in particular: "The drapes began moving as if someone was disturbing them. And yet I was alone in that room and there couldn't have been strong enough air currents to move heavy drapes. All the windows were closed and the fireplace was covered. I don't believe in ghosts. And yet why were those drapes moving without air currents?"

When Jett was about four he took a glass of water up to Eunice's room before he went to bed each night. And his father said: "The glass was always dry when I checked on it later." Maybe Jett poured out the water. But I asked him: "What does Oonie say when you bring her a glass of water?"

"She says: 'Good work!'" responded the little boy, cheerfully. "I'm about ready to quit this though because now she is asking for Kool-Aid."

One of Jett's ploys up until he was about six was to hug thin air ardently. When someone inquired about this behavior pattern he would say: "I'm hugging Oonie."

Jett is certainly a remarkable child and extremely intelligent. I'm sure he is sometimes spoofing adults when he talks of his friendship with a girl ghost. Yet she is certainly real in his active mind.

Once when he was five some workmen installed window air-conditioners in the upstairs. Jerry Jones said that the air-conditioner installed in a window of Eunice's room refused to start at first no matter what the workmen did to try and correct the trouble.

Jett was an observer. Finally, the little boy said: "Oonie is here. She's going to touch the button."

And the reluctant air-conditioner went into action although no hands were seen to touch the button. (Can it be that Jett was a sleight of hand artist at age five?)

His father told me about this incident: "Jett told those workmen so many booger stories that one of them didn't show up the next day." The little boy is fond of showing visitors through Ruth Taylor's beautifully maintained dwelling. While inspecting the front upstairs bedroom in which Lady Bird

Johnson was born, visitors often ask if any of the furnishings once belonged to the former First Lady. And Jett will reply: "If you want to see some of Lady Bird's junk you can go fifteen miles down the road to the museum at Marshall."

For years Jerry and Patricia Jones have been bantering me to spend a night in Eunice's bedroom. It had been unfurnished for years. Finally, the Joneses put a huge bed in there. And they talked me into sleeping in "that room." I only agreed if Jett would stay in there with me and introduce me to Miss Andrews.

So I took along a flashlight. And Jett and I hit the sack. I'd been horseback riding most of the day, sometimes at a gallop, and I was really tired. I went to sleep.

It must have been about midnight when Jett awakened me. The light of a full moon was coming through the transom on the huge door that led from the room to the outside upstairs gallery. I blinked in the moonlight.

Jett said: "Miss Andrews is here. She is over by the rocking chair near the door."

In the tricky moonlight it did seem that the chair was rocking. But when I turned the flashlight on the chair it was empty and not in motion.

"Miss Andrews is quick. She jumped out of the chair because she saw you aiming your light. She's over by the fireplace now," said Jett.

Every time I'd focus my flashlight to see Eunice, Jett would tell me that his friend had just moved to another part of the room. She certainly must be an agile spook.

It was clear outside yet Jett told me: "I hope it doesn't come up a storm tonight. Miss Andrews goes crazy during lightning and thunder." I think Jett would have preferred that there had been a fierce storm during my night with Eunice.

The windows on the south side of the bedroom are quite wide and about twelve feet in height. Back of the curtains are old-fashioned windup sun shades.

Suddenly one of the window shades went up, winding back to the top of its spool with sounds like a round of machine gun fire. And the drapes began to move violently. "Miss Andrews is mad," said Jett. "She is throwing a temper tantrum." I got up and rolled down the shade. It worked okay, didn't go through the windup act again.

During the following early morning hours Jett awakened me twice to tell me of Miss Andrews' comings and goings about the room. She certainly seemed a restless ghost. Jett said she admired herself in a mirror over the fireplace and again at a full-length mirror on the south side of the room.

Long about 2 A.M. there were some peculiar, shuffling sounds in the bathroom. Now we'd left the doors locked from the bathroom to the back gallery. And Jett seemed to be sound asleep. So I dashed in the bathroom, keeping in mind that someone with a key to the doors might be trying to scare me. There was no one in there. My toothbrush, on some Kleenex on a low shelf, wasn't flying around the bathroom. Maybe I imagined the strange, shuffling noises in the bathroom.

When I awoke about 6 A.M., sunshine was coming through a tear in the window shade which had gone up to the top the night before. The shade had no tear when I'd rolled it back down after midnight. I'm sure of that. And the tear was too high for Jett to have made it.

It was nice to get out in the sunshine after a night in "that room," as Angela calls it.

30

The Orange Christmas

The Christmas stuck in the synopsis of my mind happened when I was six and living with my parents on a stock farm in Roberts County, then and now one of the most sparsely settled political districts in the Texas Panhandle.

That Christmas is remembered in our family as the Orange Christmas.

My parents' place, a fragment of a big ranch owned by one of my grandfathers, was in a mural canyon with red cliffs and with willows and cottonwood trees following Red Deer Creek in the bottom of the canyon.

The Santa Fe Railroad ran down the canyon, and freight trains sometimes stopped at the switch where my father had a grain elevator.

About three days before that Christmas, a Santa Fe freight derailed and refrigerated cars turned over and scattered thousands of oranges over the right-of-way and off into perhaps five acres of one of our pastures.

Because of the grain elevator, my father had business dealings with the railroad and he usually called the division superintendent "John Santa Fe."

My father surveyed the wreck on horseback and then he rode back to the house, on a rise over the canyon, and said to my mother: "John Santa Fe says we can have all those oranges but we've got to hurry because they'll not keep. I hope this doesn't spoil our Christmas."

One of the hired hands cranked the family Marmon touring car for my mother. And before she drove off she explained:

"I'm going to get Lady Gething. She knows how to make orange marmalade."

Sir Arthur and Lady Gething were very British, although longtime residents of the Panhandle. They had a ranch about thirty miles away. My mother brought back the Gethings in midafternoon, and they got busy in the kitchen making orange marmalade and canning it and squeezing orange juice. My father had gone to the nearest towns, Miami and Pampa, and bought all the fruit jars and lids and other canning materials he could find.

And in the meantime the hired hands and Grandfather Tolbert and my uncle Weimar had been harvesting oranges, loading them into two wagons and a buggy and my grandfather's Stutz Bearcat. When my mother returned, in the Marmon touring car, the oranges were stored in our house and in the grain bins in the barn and down at the grain elevator.

Once the oranges were gathered, the menfolk helped in the kitchen with the marmalade-making and the squeezing of oranges for juice. My father was a good chuck-wagon-type cook and he had much experience making jellies and preserves from wild plums.

It was Christmas Eve when I was run off to bed, and the adults were still busy in the kitchen.

I got up about 4 A.M. The house smelled of sugar and oranges and a faint hint of mesquite smoke from the heating and cookstoves.

Everyone was asleep, except my mother, some of the visitors on pallets in the living room and dining room. My mother said she stayed up to see me open my presents.

There was a ragged old cedar from the South Canadian River brakes for a Christmas tree. It was decorated with oranges and strings of popcorn, and it looked mighty pretty to me. I tiptoed among the pallets and sleeping people to the tree.

My presents, concealed in gunnysacks, were a new bicycle and a secondhand Mexican saddle. In my Christmas stocking were some nuts—Brazil nuts, pecans, and piñons. But no oranges.

At any other Christmastime oranges were rare treats in our remote ranch country sixty-five years ago. And kids were disappointed if they didn't find oranges in their Christmas stockings. Some children never saw an orange except at Christmastime. The bright color and the smell of oranges seemed mixed up in the Christmas mystique.

My father and my grandfather knew how important an orange was to a kid at Christmas. And this was going to be the Orange Christmas throughout the 899 square miles of Roberts County. After breakfast my father and my grandfather loaded the Marmon touring car and the Stutz Bearcat with oranges. First they drove several miles down the canyon to the "section houses" where lived the Spanish-speaking workers on the railroad right-of-way. And we surprised the children there with gifts of oranges.

Then we went to all the surrounding ranch headquarters and into Miami, the only town in our county, and gave oranges to children.

Christmas dinner was ready when we got home. My mother had fried quail and made quail cream gravy with piñon nuts in the gravy. And she roasted two young wild turkey hens in the kitchen stove which was fueled with mesquite knots, and there was just a mild suggestion of chili piquins in the dressing. There were sourdough biscuits to sop in the quail cream gravy. And we had orange marmalade on the Christmas dinner, of course.

We had orange marmalade for years. We got tired of orange marmalade. But my folks never got tired of telling about the Orange Christmas. And that's why I remember it so well.

31

A Japanese Garden at the Nimitz Hotel

At big sunup on a day with a cool flavor because of spring showers I drove into Fredericksburg, Texas, and saw a sight like something in a 1920s dream. A half century after it had been torn down the wooden superstructure resembling a high out-of-the-water steamboat was back on the stone walls of the Nimitz Hotel and formed the third and fourth stories.

Actually, the Nimitz is no longer a hotel. It is now the Admiral Chester Nimitz Naval Center and Museum of the Pacific War. The towering wooden superstructure is now complete with a railed hurricane deck, simulated cabins (in the original the cabins were real), and topping it all off the reproduction of a steamboat pilot house.

Fleet Admiral Nimitz was a native of this handsome old stone town sometimes called "the German Capital of the Texas Hill Country." Admiral Nimitz's grandfather, Charles Nimitz (1826–1911) came to Fredericksburg in 1847, a year after the town was founded by a wagon train of one hundred twenty emigrants from Germany led by a red-bearded baron, Ottfried Hans von Meusebach. They made a happy settlement that is still unique.

Charles Nimitz had been a sea captain. He was responsible for the original architectural scheme of finishing off the third and fourth floors in wood to resemble sections of a steamboat above the original two floors of thick masonry. The Nimitz became one of the most popular of Texas frontier hotels, the amenities including a brewery, a bakery, good German-style food, and a wagon yard out back that was actually a fortification for it was enclosed by a high stone wall. In the late 1800s the Nimitz Hotel guests were the likes of Horace Greeley, Generals Robert E. Lee, George Custer, and Philip Sheridan, and President Rutherford B. Hayes. The high stone wall with portholes still stands but now about half of the wagon yard is taken up by a beautiful Japanese garden, built by Japanese craftsmen under the supervision of Taketora Saita, called the best garden designer in Japan.

Admiral Nimitz organized and directed the U.S. fleets that destroyed Japanese naval power in World War II. Still, in recent times a group of Japanese admirals and a former Japanese ambassador to the United States formed a committee in Japan to raise the money to build the gorgeous little garden.

Why, you ask, should the Japanese do this for their conqueror? Well, Admiral Nimitz, the great naval tactician, considered himself a disciple of the most revered of Japanese admirals, Count Heihachiro Togo (1847–1934). Togo is most remembered for his maneuvers in the Japanese-Russian War when he "crossed the T" in the Russian fleet and completely destroyed it. This happened in 1905. In that same year officers of the U.S. Asiatic fleet were invited to a party in Tokyo in the emperor's palace, honoring Admiral Togo. Captured Russian champagne was served. Midshipman Nimitz was in the U.S. party. He shook hands with Togo and told of his admiration of the admiral's genius. Whether they met again is not known but in 1934 Captain Nimitz of the flagship of the U.S. Asiatic fleet was chosen to lead an honor guard at Admiral Togo's funeral. After Nimitz's triumph in World War II some Japanese held the theory that at the 1934 funeral the "spirit" of Admiral Togo entered the body of Captain Nimitz.

In 1945, Nimitz, of course, was at the Japanese surrender ceremonies in Tokyo Bay. And the fleet admiral saved Togo's old flagship, the *Mikasha,* from destruction.

The Russians had declared war on Japan a few weeks before, just in time for the surrender ceremonies and they wanted to blow up the *Mikasha,* since it reminded them of their humiliating defeat in 1905.

Nimitz not only ordered the Russians to keep their hands off the *Mikasha,* he also started fund-raising with several hundred dollars of his own money to restore Togo's flagship. He wrote an article for Japanese newspapers urging the restoration of the *Mikasha.*

Taketora Saita, designer of the garden back of the Nimitz Hotel, said Japanese historians now rate Nimitz one of the three great admirals of all time. The others are Togo and Nelson of England.

"To show their admiration for the great Texan admiral the Japanese people raised money to build a 'Garden of Peace' in Chester Nimitz' hometown," Saita wrote.

At the north end of the classic garden there is a small Japanese house, square of design with a gabled roof and shoji screens for walls and woven tatami mats on the floor. This is a copy of Admiral Togo's study when he lived in Maizuru, Japan. A pool and stream were copied from one near Togo's study. There is a waterfall, and the trees and the pond are arranged in three dimensions.

To build the garden and the study Taketora Saita brought six Japanese craftsmen to Fredericksburg. When they arrived they were dressed in gray uniforms with the logo of Meiji Seisakusho Ltd., the contracting company, on their cap visors.

"They soon changed to western outfits," said Douglas Hubbard, director of the Nimitz Museum.

A Japanese garden needs rocks. Saita was delighted with the granite, limestone, petrified wood, and other stones that Fredericksburgers hauled in from the surrounding hills. (When Baron von Meusebach arrived at the head of the wagon train in 1846 he called these beautiful highlands "the Hills of God.") "The quality and beauty of the stones would have been difficult to find in Japan," said Saita. Then he added somewhat snobbishly: "Neither the garden nor the reproduction of Admiral Togo's study play up the Japanism which is often overdone in so-called Japanese gardens usually found in America. This is a land of springs. And by letting water flow from the upper course of the small stream we create a torrent flowing into the 'Ishin-no-ike' or 'Pond-of-one-heart.' By the beauty of this garden, the Japanese and Americans who worked together to build it hope to transform the spiritual attachment between Admiral Nimitz and Admiral Togo."

The people of Fredericksburg not only collected pretty rocks; they also contributed plants. The focal point of the garden is made by three Japanese pines, bonsai shaped. All the trees and flowering plants, while Japanese in style, are Texas grown.

It was when Saita and his craftsmen completed the study and garden that Texans learned that some Japanese believe Togo's spirit entered Nimitz's body at that funeral in Tokyo in 1934.

Nimitz died in 1966. It is too bad he didn't live to see the delicate beauty of Admiral Togo's garden reproduced behind the stone walls of the wagon yard at Grandfather Nimitz's old hotel.

32

A Beautiful Town Misspells Its Name

Downtown Granbury, Texas, is a scene of serene architectural beauty. The centerpiece is the 1890 Hood County courthouse with its classic clock tower and chocolate-colored paint trim in contrast with the scrubbed-looking exterior walls. And the courthouse is surrounded by refurbished 1800s business buildings of clean design.

There is an 1886 opera house with three hundred seats for audiences at live theater. There is a drugstore which serves ice cream in a "parlor" of antique furnishings and there is the Cherry general store. At one corner of the courthouse square is the Nutt House Hotel built in 1890 and with the decor to match. The Nutt House has a country-style dining room famous for fresh vegetables, chicken-fried steak, and water corn bread.

On the courthouse lawn there is a quaint, five-foot-high statue of a military man identified as "Brig. Gen. H. B. Granbury, C.S.A." He was the person for whom the town was named. Only trouble is his name wasn't Granbury. He was Hiram Bronson Grandberry. He died at age thirty-four leading his Texas brigade of the Confederate Army in a battle at Franklin, Tennessee, on November 30, 1864.

To check on the correct spelling I went to the Granbury cemetery on a high terrace over the Brazos River. From these heights Granbury has the look of a seaport, caught up as the town is in great coils of water backed up by the De Cordova Bend dam of the river.

After a half hour of search I'd not found the general's

grave. Then John and Lois Cavazos drove up and guided me to a thin, plain old monument. And Granbury's namesake is identified as General Grandberry on the stone.

John Cavazos said that General Grandberry was buried at first on the Tennessee battlefield. After the town had been named for him, only with the incorrect spelling, his remains were brought from Tennessee and reburied on the mesa over the Brazos.

John Cavazos is the grandson of Juan Cavazos, a prisoner of the Comanche Indians in the late 1830s or early 1840s. The wild Indians brought Juan to the trading post called Fort Spunky, operated by his brother-in-law, Charles Barnard. And Barnard bought his brother-in-law from the Comanches for trading goods. A year or so before, Charles Barnard, a canny native of Connecticut and a friend of Samuel Colt, had purchased Juan's twin sister, Juana Cavazos, from Comanche Indian bondage and married her. One story had it that Juana was bought for a sack of sugar.

The Cavazos family members today, after almost a hundred and fifty years on these shores of the Brazos, have lost most of their Hispanic traditions. Juana and Juan Cavazos were of Italian and Mexican descent.

There's nothing left of old Fort Spunky on an eastern bank of the Brazos, opposite from Granbury, except a well-tended cemetery where Juana and Charles Barnard are buried.

John and Lois Cavazos are caretakers of the Granbury cemetery. And when I was there they were upset because someone had stolen an unusual gravestone.

This marker was engraved with a likeness of two revolvers and a pair of handcuffs. And on the stone was the name, "Jesse James." It was over the grave of an old man who died in 1951 after decades of claiming that he was the outlaw, Jesse James.

33

The Oompah Band Sheriffs

Among the German colonists in the original 1846 settlement of Fredericksburg, Texas, was the Klaerner family. And there is a tradition that one of the Klaerners rode off into the Comanche country to the north, along with the colonists' scholarly leader, Baron Ottfried Hans von Meusebach. And in the Sabine River country von Meusebach and his followers made a lasting peace with the Comanches, Texas' most warlike Indians.

For decades the Klaerners were farmers. Then for about sixty of the eighty-three years from 1899 to 1982 the high sheriffs in Fredericksburg, or rather for Gillespie County, were men of the Klaerner clan. And each was also a member of Fredericksburg's oompah band.

The latest of these was Hugo Klaerner, a onetime pitcher for the Chicago White Sox baseball team. He was known as "Cousin Hugo" for the thirty years he was sheriff, and he died shortly after serving his last term. He was proud that in all those thirty years as a peace officer he never used his gun in line of duty, except once when he fired a warning shot in the air.

Cousin Hugo inherited a musical instrument he called an "alto" from his father, Alfred (Smoky) Klaerner, sheriff for all but two terms from 1918 to 1943. The alto is a kind of trumpet and is no longer manufactured. Smoky Klaerner also played the tuba. From 1899 to 1911, Hugo's uncle, John Klaerner, was sheriff and tuba player in the oompah band now named in honor of a retired musician, Fritz Pehl.

The oompah band plays for dances and at weddings and at the annual chili cook-off in the Gillespie County village of Luckenbach. Luckenbach is an old (1850) Indian trading post celebrated in the Waylon Jennings-Willie Nelson hit song of several seasons past. The village, with an 1850 store as the centerpiece, is the scene each October of the Texas State Chili Cook-off for Women Only, sponsored by an aggressive organization called The Hell Hath No Fury Chili Society. The society was founded in 1972 by a Dallas woman, Mickey Trent, with advice from Alex Burton of Dallas radio station KRLD (who named the group "Hell Hath No Fury etc.") and Frank Tolbert. We tried to get the first cook-off in the Texas towns of Queen City, Hearne, and Lovelady but were turned down. Finally, the owners of Luckenbach, Hondo Crouch and Guich Koock, agreed to be the hosts.

Women under ninety years of age are barred from competing in the annual Texas State Chili Cook-off in San Marcos, called the Republic of Texas Chilimpiad. The fellows who run the men's cook-off believe the philosophy of George Haddaway, one of the founders of the Chili Appreciation Society International in 1933, 1949, or 1951. (No one seems to remember the exact year.) Haddaway won't let women attend meetings of his First Dallas Pod (chapter) of CASI. This is in tune with the philosophy of H. Allen Smith, a contestant in the original chili cook-off, the 1967 World Championship at Terlingua, who wrote: "No one should be permitted to cook chili while then and there being a female person." (The San Marcos chauvinists relented a bit in recent times and now permit women over ninety years of age to compete for the state title.)

Getting back to the Fritz Pehl band, these musicians frequently perform at multi-keg weddings in the Hill Country. Among these fun-loving folks a wedding is judged by the number of kegs of beer served. Any girl can be proud of a ten-keg wedding or better.

The presence of a sheriff in a band discouraged uncivilized behavior at dances in Gillespie County. Smoky Klaerner set a pattern. He would put down his trumpet (alto) and collar the person or persons causing a disturbance. He would take the offender or offenders outside. Being handcuffed to a tree was the usual punishment. The penitent ones would be released after the dance.

Hugo Klaerner, a formidable athlete, said he seldom had to use his father's disciplinarian methods at dances. I wondered how he performed for thirty years as a sheriff without using his gun except for that one shot in the air. I asked a Fredericksburg old-timer about this and he said: "Cousin Hugo didn't need a gun. I was once hit by his fists and it was like being kicked in the face by a mule. His papa, Smoky, and his uncle John were pretty handy with their fists, too, I understand."

Smoky Klaerner was sheriff when alcoholic beverages were outlawed in the United States.

"As far as beer and wine were concerned, there was never much prohibition in Gillespie County. And nobody sneaked around about it," Hugo Klaerner told me.

He said that Smoky Klaerner usually heard from officers in adjoining counties when federal liquor control officers were headed for Gillespie County. Smoky would call all the beer brewers and wine makers in the county and recite a warning in the German language: "Die Kühe auf der Wiede" or "The cows are in the pasture."

The Klaerners were versatile musicians. For example, Hugo, in addition to trumpet and tuba, also played the guitar, accordion, E-flat cornet, and snare drums.

One of the good places to hear the oompah band when you are in town is Oma Koock's (Grandma Koock's) restaurant owned by Guich Koock, and with the menu supervised by Guich's mother, Mary Faulk Koock.

34

Winning Wasn't Anything

If Coach Stewart Ferguson ever used an Arkansas farkle stick as a good luck talisman it was with the fervent hope that his Arkansas A & M football team, called the Boll Weevils, would lose yet another game.

Ferguson had been the winningest coach in its history for five years at his alma mater, Dakota Wesleyan. At Arkansas A & M (now the University of Arkansas at Monticello) though, this friendly fellow, also a full professor with a Ph.D., had his head full of a new and unique coaching philosophy, one that hinged on failure of a sort.

He agreed to a three-year contract to coach the Boll Weevils only after it had been spelled out that he didn't have to win a single game. In fact, the wording in his contract suggested that losing football games was his aim, providing the Boll Weevils had fun doing it.

He was, of course, considered a wild eccentric, even dangerous by some opposing coaches with a win-or-else attitude.

Even more strange to other coaches he insisted that his athletes not be given any financial aid.

Even after his contract had been publicized, followers of the Weevils weren't prepared for their players' new weird ways on the gridiron, such as driving down the field to the opponent's one-yard line and then, on the next play, have the punter for Arkansas A & M whirl around and kick the ball back upfield in the direction of the Boll Weevil goal line.

"Above all," Stewart Ferguson declared, "football must be fun. We'll trade a laugh for a touchdown any day."

What private vision drove Ferguson and his football squads may never be known, but the coach did admit that the Boll Weevils were the instruments of his aim to "ridicule and satirize high-pressure collegiate football." He wanted "to give the game back to the boys."

The "boys" on Ferguson's first Weevil squad were not always typical athletes. They included a thirty-eight-year-old Methodist preacher, the town barber in Monticello, Arkansas, and a former cheerleader whom Ferguson transformed into a passer. There were also a number of really gifted athletes, several of them acrobats and gymnasts, and two who had won collegiate wrestling titles. They were doubtless good enough to have won most of the thirty-three games they played through this era, but Ferguson's men were never ones to let victory get in the way of success. And so, from 1939 to 1941, their record was three wins, thirty losses, and no ties—a triumph of imagination over incentive.

"We had to work hard to lose some of those games," recalled John Scritchfield of Austin, Texas, who played halfback, guard, center, and end on all three of Ferguson's squads. They also had to go a long way to lose. Ferguson loved to travel, and he planned the Weevil schedule so that only five games were played at home while he coached at A & M. For the rest, the Weevils journeyed as far as California, Pennsylvania, and South Dakota. In light of their record, this arrangement might seem more self-protective than desired, but Ferguson just thought travel would broaden his men. As for the games played once the Weevils got there, things occasionally turned downright absurd. The team was frightfully casual about scoring touchdowns. "Just when we were on the lip of the enemy goal and about to score," Scritchfield said, "we'd go into our 'London Bridge Is Falling Down' formation—that is, the whole team would just fall flat—or 'Red England'—one of our punters would whirl and kick the ball back downfield."

Scritchfield, who later was the first-string quarterback for Georgia Pre-Flight, a service team that remained unbeaten and had four All-Americas on its roster, said Ferguson didn't actually discourage touchdowns. "Sometimes he'd let us score early just to unnerve the opposition," he recalled. One maneuver that Ferguson instituted probably did more than unnerve the opposition. J. P. Leveritt, a halfback, perfected a play in which he would walk on his hands for a touchdown with the football clutched between his legs. Once he hand-walked in from the fifteen-yard line.

"It certainly upset the other team to give up six points to a ballcarrier walking on his hands," said Scritchfield. "The other side would figure at that point we were going to give them a bad whipping. After one of those walk-in touchdowns we might drive right down to the goal line again, but then we'd revert to our losing style. In one game against a Pennsylvania college, we scored that way, then drove to their five-yard line on the next series. But instead of running it over, we huddled and made up a play involving nineteen successive laterals that carried us back to our own ten."

Ferguson's ambition to lose all his games eluded him until his final season at A & M. He failed in 1939 when his team played one of its two home games of the year and beat Northwest Mississippi College 26–6. In the 1940 campaign the Weevils nearly found themselves humiliated, beating both Northwest Mississippi and the South Dakota School of Mines. But his 1941 team, which he called his masterpiece, managed to lose all twelve of its games. To achieve this inverted perfection he had to make adjustments in the schedule, scratching off the South Dakota and the Mississippi teams as being simply too inept.

Some sportswriters and coaches who didn't understand Ferguson's motivations pictured him as either crazy or a man who hated football. Neither assessment was correct. If anything, he loved football too much to willingly accept the excesses of overemphasis. He had been a successful college player, achieving Little All-America honors as an end at Dakota Wesleyan, and for five years prior to taking on the Arkansas A & M job, and as previously mentioned, he had been the winningest coach in the history of his alma mater. There he was regarded as an authority on scoring from within the ten-yard line, and he even wrote an article on the subject for the *Athletic Journal.*

From Dakota Wesleyan he moved on to A & M, where in addition to his duties as dean of men, he was coach and athletic director and an instructor in psychology, biology, and medieval history. Prior to his arrival, the school had been subsidizing football for years, yet had lost most of its games and much money. They were about to abandon the sport when Ferguson proposed his "simon-pure" program. All he wanted was a strict "no-win" policy from administration and alumni and great latitude in preparing road schedules.

The majority of the squad he assembled were phys-ed majors, but Ferguson had other A & M professors block out courses of study for the footballers during their long road trips. The coach would hold classes daily and would supervise study periods. He often got permission for the Weevils to attend classes at colleges along the way. Southern Cal, Notre Dame, Yale, and Hofstra were just a few of the schools where his players occasionally audited.

His music majors managed to attend operas and concerts in large cities. His agriculture majors took soil samples all over the country. Art and history majors hit big-time galleries and historical sites. The Boll Weevils of 1939–1941 were a kind of road-company lyceum. And during those three seasons, the football players made better grades on the average than their stay-at-home classmates.

Meanwhile, they were endearing themselves to football fans all over the country. Bored with the reverence paid to winning teams and winning coaches, many people found this troupe of eccentrics refreshing relief. The New York *Times* reported: "If other coaches would follow Professor Ferguson's coaching philosophy, football might be returned to the sanity of its early days." The Los Angeles *Times* crusaded unsuccessfully to have A & M play another group of "pure amateurs" in a preliminary game before the 1940 Rose Bowl contest.

Their flattering notices in the press (one journal dubbed them the "Marx Brothers of football") gave the Arkansas squad a spirited box office. Despite the expenses of bumping around the nation in a bus, the Weevils showed a profit in each of Ferguson's three seasons.

Not all of the A & M shenanigans occurred on field. A six-foot, seven-inch pass-catching gymnast named Lawrence (The Stork) Lavender was occasionally dolled up before games in a bobtailed dress coat, starched white shirtfront, and white tie over the game jersey, and wearing gloves, a silk top hat, and sometimes a monocle. A "valet" helped him dress.

The A & M colors were green and white, yet the squad took along road jerseys of many colors, and Ferguson let the players wear any combination they wished. Sometimes the team changed colors at halftime, even emerging in jerseys of the same color as the other team.

As long as his players were behaving themselves, Ferguson exerted no real control over them during a game. Each was allowed to take any position he wished, and substitutions were at the whim of the players themselves. Subs rode a bicycle from bench to field, and the replaced player rode it back. Players were free to leave the bench and join friends in the stands. One of the better ballcarriers, Bix Stillwell, was also a spectacular drummer. He would take himself out of games and sit in with the opposing team's band at odd moments, sometimes, according to John Scritchfield, getting long ovations from the fans for his drum solos.

"I enjoyed the games each of those seasons because I could sit on the sidelines and wonder what my players were going to do next," Ferguson reminisced afterward. So, no doubt, did the Weevils' fans and opposition.

J. S. Shapiro, who sometimes played halfback, rarely wore shoes in a game, even in northern snow. An extra-point attempt by either team in a Weevil game was apt to be traumatic. On tries by the opponent, all the Weevils frequently collapsed to the turf on the snap from center, causing the startled kicker to boot the ball wide of the uprights. If A & M scored, the point-after could be equally bizarre. Some of the Weevil players would line up with their backsides to the other team. Then the placekicker would do something awkward, like missing the football and booting the ball holder, usually an acrobat, who would then do a series of backflips over the goal line. Bear Bryant would have cried.

Ferguson could be a tough disciplinarian. The Weevils were drilled long hours on fundamentals and spent still more time at calisthenics and gymnastics, so they were always in unusually good condition. Not one serious injury hit the Weevils in his three seasons. Ferguson squads always behaved like gentlemen. At hotels and motels where they stayed, managers praised their behavior, in contrast with other visiting teams.

Ferguson went into the service in 1942 and never returned to Arkansas A & M. When he died in 1955 he had been the football coach at Deadwood (South Dakota) High ten years, and his obituary said: "The fifty-five-year-old coach won fame for himself at Arkansas A & M by practicing the theory that a football team doesn't have to win games to provide entertainment for the fans and fun for the players. He used much the same coaching tactics at Deadwood High."

Once when his 1941 Boll Weevils were to play a game with Bradley University in Peoria, Illinois (the Weevils lost 67–0), Ferguson told a group of sportswriters: "You fellows laugh at my boys when they're losing on Saturdays. Yet for the rest of the week they're learning more, absorbing more culture and social graces than any other football squad in this nation."

UNDER THE
FARKLEBERRY
TREE

35

The Great Farkles

Zavalla, population about 800, is a village in the Angelina National Forest in Texas' heaviest producer of commercial timber, Angelina County. (The hamlet honors Dr. Justiniano de Zavala [one "1"], 1789–1836, first vice-president of the Republic of Texas, and Angelina is for a female chief of the Hainai Indians in the early 1700s.)

Seventy percent of Angelina County is said to be in commercial forests, mostly pine, but with some hardwoods and a few farkleberries. Off a few miles southwest of Zavalla down Farm Road 1270 and along the Poland Cemetery Road, there are several of the largest farkleberry trees in the United States, some as much as twenty-nine feet in height.

The farkleberry's botanical manual name is *Vaccinium arboreum* Marsh, Farkleberry or Sparkleberry. Dr. Cyrus Longworth Lundell of the University of Texas at Dallas' botanical laboratory is the leading authority on the giant Texas farkles. In recent years some Californians have organized a sort of a farkleberry appreciation club. However, Dr. Lundell says that farkles don't flourish in California. In fact, the trees with the sparkling personality are found mostly in sandy soils and in pine forests, frequently along wooded streams, but only in a territory from Texas to Florida and as far north as South Dakota and Virginia.

The sparkling leaves may be one reason that believers in the magic of Mojo Hand adopted the farkle as a talisman. The trees or shrubs need some shade to really sparkle, otherwise they will just frizzle before they farkle. So the farkles love the companionship of larger trees, especially pine.

In 1982 Dr. Lundell was asked by some California horticulturists to provide them with wild Texas farkleberry trees for experimental use as rootstock for cultivated blueberries. This would be done to make the cultivated blueberries more healthful and hardy, same as wild grape rootstock has been grafted to improve the vigor of cultivated grapes. (A Texan, Dr. Thomas Volney Munson, of Denison, used wild Texas grapes as rootstock to save the vineyards of Europe from total destruction by the plant louse called grape phylloxera. For this service in the 1890s, France gave the Texas viticulturist its highest award, Chevalier de la Légion d'Honneur.)

Now the farkleberry is not considered a commercial tree. There may be farkle farming, though, if there is demand for rootstock.

In 1982 Texas a mild demand was created for dried farkleberries. Couples about to be married asked that dried farkleberries be thrown at weddings rather than the traditional rice. This happened after I wrote in my Dallas *News* column that Mr. and Mrs. Roger Jones of Wichita Falls believed that their marriage, the second for both, has been a happy one partly because the lucky berries were thrown at their wedding in March 1977, in Tolbert's Native Texas Foods and Museum of the Chili Culture in downtown Dallas.

That season a sparkling farkleberry tree had been used as a Christmas tree at the Tolbert cafe and chili museum. The berries on the tree had dried by the time of the Jones wedding. Kathleen Tolbert and Frank Tolbert No. 2 gathered handfuls of the dried berries and tossed them on the Joneses as they were leaving.

Mr. and Mrs. Jones returned to the cafe-museum in April 1982. They said that the farkleberry-throwing somehow had a magic effect on their marriage. Mr. Jones, an assistant football coach in 1977, had become a successful businessman and they had a beautiful, two-year-old girl child, Jodi Jones.

I wrote in my Dallas *News* column about the Joneses' faith in farkleberries. The column got me invitations to weddings. So far I have thrown the berries at thirty weddings including those of the following friends: Billie Branch Moziek, Elizabeth Ann Weichsel Galvis, Nan Neale Bryant, Susan Ziller Brazzell, and Karen Arrington Jordan.

Spring should be the prime time for throwing farkleberries at weddings. The trees are especially handsome then, graced, in addition to essentially evergreen and lustrous leathery leaves, with spicy-smelling, bell-shaped white flowers.

The Spaniards, when first they came to Texas, mentioned "the tree that sparkled."

It is fitting that the biggest farkles are in Angelina County, in the Angelina National Forest, and near the Angelina River. For all of these landmarks were named for a remarkable Indian woman who lived in this same country from about 1670 to 1750. She was called Angelina by the Spanish and Angelique in the chronicles of French explorers.

Angelina was a member of a tribe of the Hasinai-Caddo Confederacy, the Hainai. According to Gaspar de Solis, a Spanish priest, the Hainai women were a liberated group. The padre wrote that "a Hainai woman known as Santa Adiva (not Angelina) is the great or principal lady. She receives gifts from other tribes. She has five husbands and is, in a word, like a queen among them."

Solis said that the "principal Hainai women" carried "wands of wood that sparkled" and sometimes beat their husbands with these instruments.

Angelina may also have beaten her husbands with a farkleberry club. The Spanish were impressed with her beauty and intelligence. When she was quite young, she was taken with a Spanish entrada across Texas to the San Juan Bautista mission on the Rio Grande (near present-day Piedras Negras, Mexico, and Eagle Pass, Texas). She lived at the mission for about two years and was educated in the Spanish language.

In 1713 a party of Frenchmen, led by Louis Juchereau de

St. Denis, entered the Hainai country. The French governor of
Louisiana, Antoine de la Mothe Cadillac (after whom the automobile is named), had entrusted St. Denis with opening a
trade route with the Spaniards to the Rio Grande. Actually, St.
Denis was also trying to assert a French claim to Texas, for in
one communication he said that this land between the Sabine
and the Rio Grande would be called the Province of Cadillac,
in honor of the Louisiana governor. A member of the St.
Denis expedition wrote: "In this Hainai village we found a
woman called Angelique. She spoke Spanish very well. And as
St. Denis was familiar with that language he employed her as
an interpreter."

Angelina could be called "the Pocahontas of Texas" for in
1719 she saved a young French explorer, François Simars de
Bellise, from being burned at the stake by the Hainai.

Angelina or Angelique, "the angelic one," could be a little
devil.

After saving the handsome aristocrat from the fire, she
turned him into one of her slavelike husbands, complete with
hard work and regular beatings with her farkle wand.

Angelina made her last appearance in written records on
July 3, 1720, when she was among the Hainai dignitaries who
gave a chamber of commerce kind of welcome to the great
Spanish expedition led by the Marquis de Aguayo, governor
and captain-general of the provinces of Coahuila and Texas.
The expedition drove the French from Texas and reestab-
lished the missions in eastern Texas. The previous year the
Spanish priests had fled to San Antonio because of the aggres-
sions of the French from Louisiana bent on establishing the
Province of Sieur Cadillac.

And what happened to Angelina's slave-husband, the
Frenchman de Bellise? He wrote a letter addressed "to the first
white man," complaining that he was being beaten regularly
by his Indian wife and forced to do menial work, and entrusted it to an Indian who was going to Louisiana. Incredibly,
the letter reached St. Denis in New Orleans, and he paid some

members of another Indian nation to kidnap Angelina's prisoner. De Bellise eventually became a leading citizen of New Orleans.

It is easy to imagine Angelina standing before the Marquis de Aguayo on July 3, 1720, perhaps on one of the ceremonial mounds of the Hainai. For Father Espinosa, the marquis' diarist, wrote: "On the third day of July an Indian woman of this same nation, well versed in both languages, served as interpreter. On this day the cacique of the nation of Hainais, who all the nations of Texas recognize as their superior, arrived with the principal Indians, among them Angelina . . ."

And Father Solis wrote: "The Rio de Angelina takes its name from a Texas Indian woman who was very useful to us because of both her knowledge of languages and the good offices she recommended to her countrymen . . ."

Was it their farkle wands' magic which kept the Hainai women from being slaves like most other females in wild Indian tribes?

Anyway, it seems fitting that the biggest farkle trees in the United States and possibly in the world are in a national forest named for this pioneer "libber," this matriarch who whipped her husbands with a farkleberry limb.

36

Awesome Power of the Arkansas Farkle

The farkleberry is only a shrub in Arkansas. And yet Arkansas folks are probably more aware of farkle power than are Texans.

"The farkleberry has become an institution in Arkansas," wrote George Fisher of Little Rock, a talented cartoonist and author. "Everyone around here knows the wild razorback feeds on farkleberries. Hence his awesome power. We know farkleberries grow higher in Texas. And we are fearful that Texans may become fully aware of the power of the fruit of the farkle."

George Fisher drew and wrote a book about Orval Faubus, five times the governor of Arkansas. And the book's cover is a cartoon of Governor Faubus and a farkleberry bush atop the state capitol.

Faubus was so intimately connected with the farkle that Fisher titles his last chapter "The Fall of the Farkleberry." This final chapter tells of Faubus' defeat on his sixth try to be reelected as governor.

In his preface Fisher suggests that Faubus' love of the farkle was a secret affair until a certain incident happened on an Arkansas highway: "A woman motorist driving down a road in Franklin County did a double take and stopped her car when she saw a crew of men working alongside the road in a clump of farkleberries."

For one of the laborers was a man in stained khaki who was quite familiar to the woman motorist. Governor Faubus had pitched in to help the crew clear underbrush along the road.

He wanted to make sure this work was done without damaging ornamental trees such as the farkleberries.

George Fisher wrote: "Since then the words 'farkleberry' and 'Faubus' have been synonymous."

37

Psychiatrists Love Farkles

Florida had the biggest farkleberry tree until 1967. Then the superior giants were discovered in Texas and called to the attention of the National Forestry Association.

Even though they're No. 2 now, Florida folks still appreciate their farkles. In fact, Dr. Stanley Dean, a Miami, Fla., psychiatrist, is the inventor of that wonderful new cocktail, the farkletini. This a normal dry vodka or gin martini except that zestful flavor has been added by a farkleberry as the garnish instead of the cliché olive.

Farkletinis are beginning to catch on in bars across the country, such as at some Marriott Hotel lounges when the berries are in season, and at Tolbert's in Dallas. And there is a Farkleberry Lounge in College Station, Texas.

Dr. Dean got the idea for the drink in Dallas in April 1972. He was at an annual national gathering of the American College of Psychiatrists. And in Dallas that April more than three hundred psychiatrists from all over the nation learned about the farkle.

In fact, farkleberries were sort of the theme of the national meeting.

Dr. Perry Talkington of Dallas was president of the American College of Psychiatrists that year and of course the host at the meeting.

Months before, he had asked me to help him arrange for more than three hundred sprigs of fresh farkles in bloom to be delivered in Dallas on the last day of the psychiatrists' convention. The idea was to put a sprig of farkles in flower by the plate of each shrink at the final dinner. Doc Talkington wanted each psychiatrist to leave Dallas with a good Mojo Hand.

Now Albert and Elizabeth Agnor have the biggest farkleberry plantation in Texas, and probably the hemisphere. They make farkleberry jelly and wine, and Albert even puts farkleberries in chili con carne. In 1975 he won the World Championship Chili Cook-off at Arriba Terlingua with his farkle chili.

The Agnors agreed to supply Dr. Talkington with his farkleberry order.

The day before the psychiatrists' big dinner in Dallas, Albert and Elizabeth harvested about four hundred sprigs when the flowers were in their most glorious, white bell-shaped state. The sprigs were soaked in water for about two hours and then packed with crushed ice in waxlike poultry containers.

The flowers were as fresh as if they'd just been gathered at the Agnors' Millstone Farm when the sprigs were placed by each guest's plate at the Fairmount Hotel, and the great hall was fragrant with the spicy smell of farkles in bloom.

The principal speaker that night was Bob Murphey, a tobacco-chewing lawyer who lives on a grand estate near the village of Looneyville in Nacogdoches County.

I didn't figure that Bob could resist telling the psychiatrists that Looneyville is near Little Loco Creek, "and you fellows ought to hold your next convention in Looneyville."

Murphey didn't talk much about psychiatry that evening though. He did some philosophizing on politicians in Washington: "They're just like cockroaches. It's not what they eat and tote away, it's what they fall in."

He told about a backcountry fellow who took his hound dog along when he went to the Looneyville bank to try and borrow some money.

The Looneyville banker refused the loan. The country fellow turned to his dog and said: "Sic him!" The hound bit the banker and then ran out in the bank lobby and started biting customers.

The banker was indignant. He said to the country fellow: "I can understand why you had your dog bite me. I turned you down. But I can't understand why you let your dog bite my customers."

"Oh, I didn't tell him to bite your customers," said the country fellow. "Biting the customers is his idea. He's trying to get the banker taste out of his mouth."

He did get back to the subject of the sprigs at each plate: "I knew you psychiatrists needed something. And your host, Dr. Talkington, knew what it was, some farkleberries."

A day or so later I got a note from Dr. Talkington: "The Agnors came through bountifully with the farkleberries. Bob Murphey was both a delight personally and as an after-dinner speaker. The combination made for a truly memorable evening. I am grateful for your help."

Sarah Greene said that "Dr. Talkington has a ranch near Gilmer heavily planted in farkles. He probably doesn't know he has all those beautiful little trees or he wouldn't have bothered you and the Agnors."

Sarah and her husband, Ray, own and edit and manage the Gilmer Daily *Mirror* in Gilmer, Texas, and Sarah raises farkles in the yard of the Greene manse.

She has written essays in praise of the farkle, such as this excerpt from one:

"By late November the scissor-tailed flycatchers have stripped the persimmon trees of their sugar plums and the grapevines have long since been finally denuded by the foxes. The raccoons are eating the last of the French mulberries and the crows have gotten all the unguarded pecans. But all is not bleak for the little creatures of the East Texas forests. For the farkleberries are still there and will be there for the rest of the winter."

The earliest scientific studies of the Florida and Texas farkles that I've seen were made by Dr. Charles Sprague Sargent, an 1862 graduate of Harvard University. Starting in 1873 and for several decades he was director of the Arnold Arboretum at Harvard. Dr. Sprague said that the berries of the farkle "sometimes persist on the branches until the end of winter. And so the berries are important in the food cycles of wild birds."

He said farkle wood is very close-grained and hard, ideal for clubs and for the handles of tools, such as axes. He said East Texas Indians in the old days used "decoctions of the astringent bark of the root and of the leaves in a treatment of diarrhea." He said the fruit ripens in October "and is of a slightly astringent yet pleasant flavor."

A book called *Guide to Southern Trees,* published by Whittlesay House, devotes three pages to the farkle. The guide declares that farkle wood has been used for making tobacco pipes and woodware, and the bark is suitable for tanning leather. It is also claimed that South Dakota is the northernmost state planted in farkles, and these are usually shrubs.

I am quoting this authority because Red Fenwick, who writes a saddlesore column for the Denver *Post* called "Riding the Range," wrote that there is an annual Farkleberry Festival in South Dakota "in Gordon Hanson's old hometown, Hayti, S.D., and this is the biggest time of the year in Hayti. Farkleberries grow on trees in Texas and Florida but on bushes in South Dakota. There's some dispute as to who raises the best farkles. Personally, I prefer South Dakota farkleberries. The Dakota farkleberries are more succulent."

Dr. Cyrus Longworth Lundell of Dallas is at once the leading authority on the botany of Guatemala and also the discoverer of many archaeological wonders in that country. Once when I was on a mule trip in the Guatemala jungles with Dr. Lundell, he became the first to find and identify a Central American version of the farkleberry. He named it in my honor because, as Dr. Lundell phrased it, "Tolbert is a farkle freak." The plant is listed in latest manuals on the botany of Gua-

temala as *Vaccinium tolbertium* Lundell, farkleberry or sparkleberry . . .

Unfortunately, Dr. Lundell is not much of a fan of the farkle. "Farkles are strictly for the birds. I realize their impor-
tance for birds and small mammals who are desperate for food
at the tail end of winter. But for human beings the berries are
too dry to bother with. You need a lot of time to make wine or
jelly from those berries."

38

Why the Farkle Failed to Become Texas' State Berry

Albert Agnor, owner of the largest farkle farm in East Texas, and I persuaded Ben Z. Grant, a member of the state legislature from Marshall, to introduce two bills in a regular session of the Texas' lawmakers. One was to honor chili con carne as the official state dish. The other bill proposed the farkleberry as the official state berry.

Well, Ben Z. Grant earned a place in chili culture history and also in the annals of unusual legislation by his success in making chili con carne the state dish. He failed with the farkleberries, this despite some brilliant oratory by Mr. Grant and other East Texas legislators. It did no good to point out that Texas has the tallest farkles in the United States and perhaps in the world.

"I just couldn't get that farkle bill out of committee," Grant reported to Agnor and me. And some West Texas lawmakers ganged up on me, members of the "mulberry mafia" and those under influence of the "strawberry lobby."

I'm a West Texas native and I told Ben Grant that the lawmakers from my part of the state were probably against his berry bill because farkleberries don't flourish in West Texas. Out there the blueberry trees lack the companionship and shade of pine trees except in the Trans-Pecos mountains and even these trees seldom sparkle. In fact they frizzle before they can farkle.

Dr. Stanley Dean of Miami, Florida, one of the psychiatrists who attended the meeting in Dallas when each delegate got a fresh sprig of farkleberries, said that he believed the West

Texas legislators who defeated Ben Grant's berry bill were probably suffering from a syndrome called "farkle jealousy."

Dr. Dean said that after his state was found to have smaller farkleberry trees than those in Texas some Floridians, knowledgeable about the trees, also suffered from "farkle jealousy."

Psychiatrists certainly haven't forgotten farkles since their 1972 convention in Dallas. The official publication of the American College of Psychiatrists has published recipes for farkleberry jelly and wines and for farkle soup. And in a letter to Dr. Gene L. Usdin of New Orleans and printed in the ACP's publication, Dr. Dean wrote:

"I have discovered the most remarkable concoction of our age—the farkletini. The other night Marion (his wife) and I were drinking ordinary dry martinis with Beefeater gin. Then this wonderful thing happened. On impulse I dropped some green farkleberries in my martini. Immediately green tears oozed from the berries. The tearful farkleberries imparted to my martini a dimension of soul never experienced before in this usually mundane drink. The farkletini was born! Never again will an ordinary martini taste the same. I eschew any thought of profit or gain. I donate this fabulous discovery to the American College of Psychiatrists!"

The peatini, with a pickled black-eyed pea replacing the olive or farkleberry, is popular in East Texas. Bill Perryman, the Athens, Texas, oilman previously mentioned for his prowess as a washpot stew cook, claims he invented the peatini before Dr. Dean conceived his farkletini. Neither has applied for a trademark. Once at the Black-eyed Pea Cook-off in Athens, Agnor made some farkletinis and said he would match them against Perryman's pea-flavored martini. I assembled a jury. Dolly Deibel, Chantal Westerman, Imogene Twitty, Dick Hitt, Bill Murchison, Jack Brown, Chip Moody, Jim Redd, Paul D. Smith, Grant Victor, Bryan Woolley, and Trisha O'Keefe were sworn in. And these experts tested several cold pitchers of peatinis and farkletinis. After all the peatinis and farkletinis, though, the jury persons became very indecisive.

The *Texas Parks* magazine, a handsome state publication, was graced in 1973 by a beautiful watercolor painting of a tufted titmouse sitting in a farkleberry tree. The painting was by an Austin artist, Nancy McGowan Pruitt, and it showed the fat, lively little bird with many green farkleberries also in view, the berries at the stage Dr. Dean recommends them for his farkletinis.

The painting illustrated a story about how a farmer owned the tree which the tufted titmouse favored for roosting. The highway department was putting in a new farm road and wanted to cross the property with the road and chop down the farkleberry tree. The farmer protested so strongly that the highway department changed the route of the road. Apparently the farmer didn't want his name used in the story. Nor was the location of the farm given. So I don't know who the heroic farmer was, nor do I know whether he was really trying to protect the titmouse more than the tree. Tufted titmice are lovable little birds.

A Dallas bird expert, Ned Fritz, told me that since the tufted titmouse doesn't migrate and stays in Texas all winter, the bird appreciates and eats a lot of farkleberries on the shank end of the winter. (As written before in this narrative, farkleberries cling to the limbs more stubbornly than any other berries and are often still there for the taking after all other such foodstuffs are gone.)

Don MacLean of United Feature Syndicate, writing in a column from England, suggested that the Angelina National Forest in East Texas be changed to the Farkleberry National Forest.

His address then was No. 3 Walden House, 32 Marylebone High Street, London, WI, England. I wrote him I was very much opposed to his suggestion. Angelina, the lovely Hainai Indian of the late 1600s and early 1700s, deserved to have a national forest named for her. And not just because she had five husbands. I am determined that this honor shall not be taken from her just because her forests happen to contain the real giants of the farkle kingdom.

MacLean had an alternative suggestion. He said a public recreation area in the grove of the largest of the trees in Angelina County should be fenced in and the area designated as the Farkle State Park.

"Sounds romantic," said MacLean.

I have not given up on getting the farkleberry recognized as the official state berry. A committee to lobby for the berry beloved by the nation's psychiatrists and other tree fanciers has been appointed and consists of Albert Agnor, Ben Z. Grant (no longer in the legislature), Calvin Clyde, Jr., Bill Newkirk, Governor Joe Sierra of the Tigua Indian Pueblo, former Texas Governor Bill Clements, David Dean, Lee Cullum, Stanley Marsh No. 3, Stanley Marcus, Thom Marshall, Bill Porterfield.